Look to the House of the Lord

Pictures of the Logan LDS Temple,

in Logan, Utah.

C. A. AYRES

ISBN: 1544968515
ISBN-13: 978-1544968513

One thing have I desired of the LORD, that will I seek after; that I may dwell in the house of the LORD all the days of my life, to behold the beauty of the LORD, and to inquire in his temple.

Psalm 27:4

Logan LDS Temple, Logan, Utah

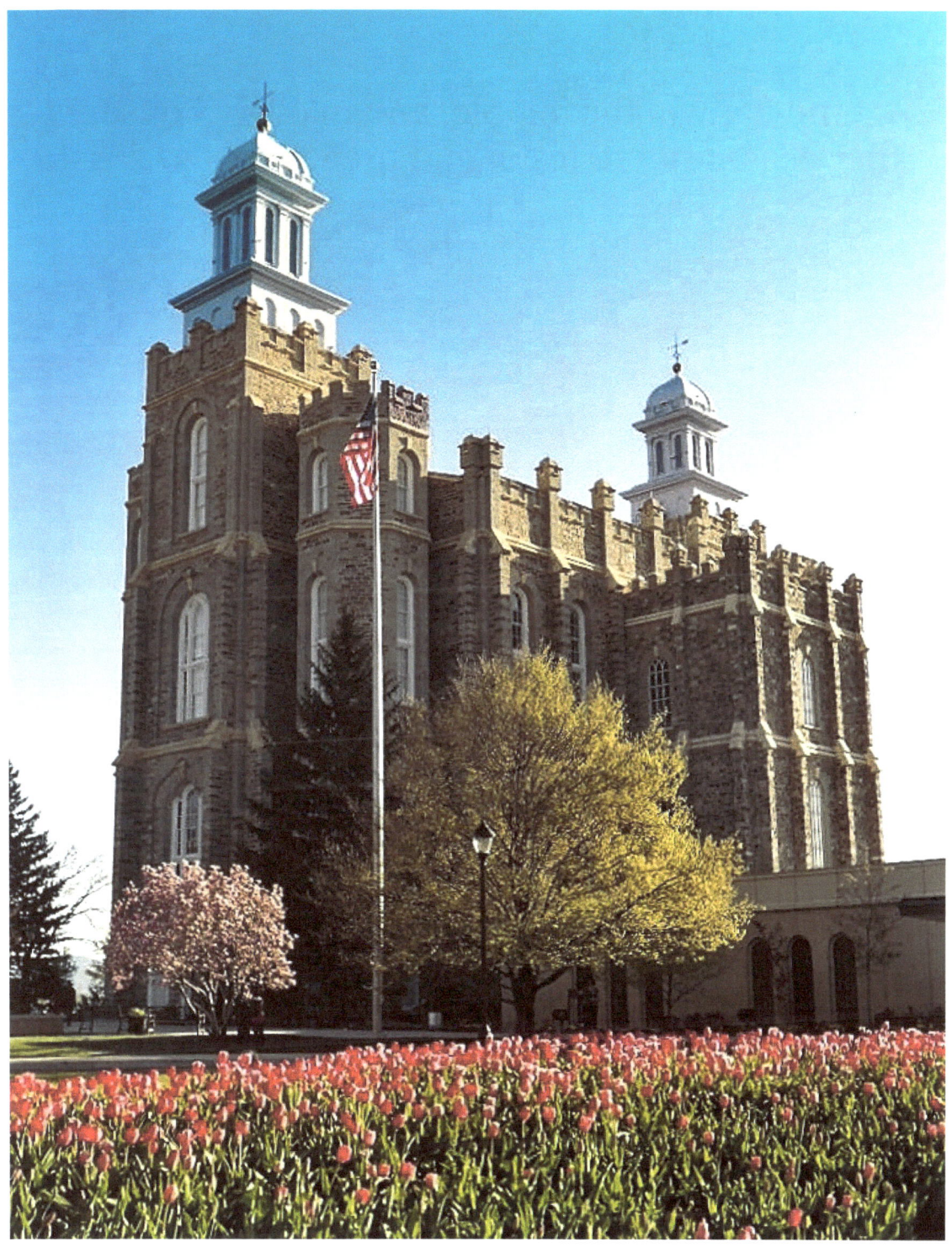

And daily in the temple, and in every house,
they ceased not to teach and preach Jesus Christ.

Acts 5:42

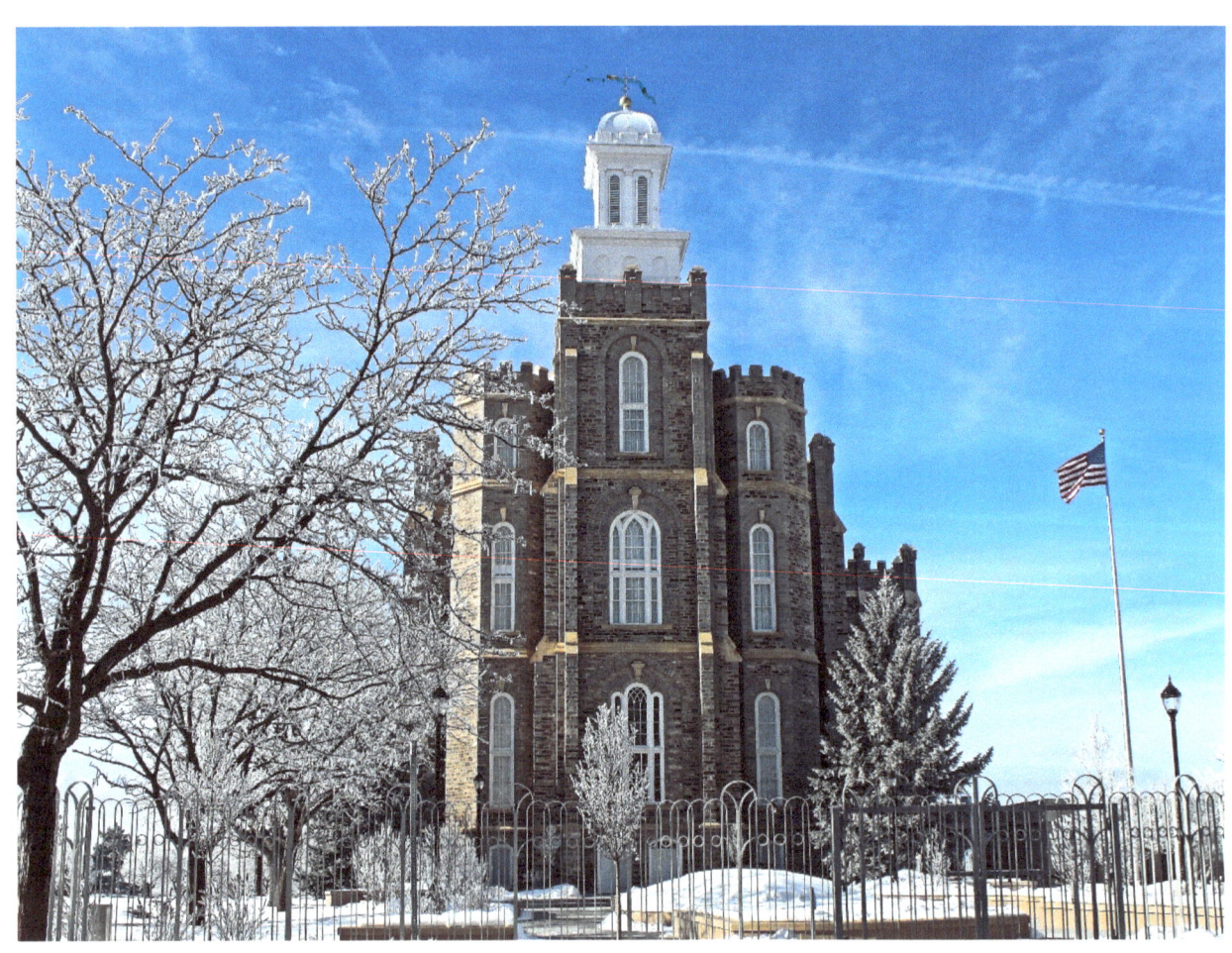

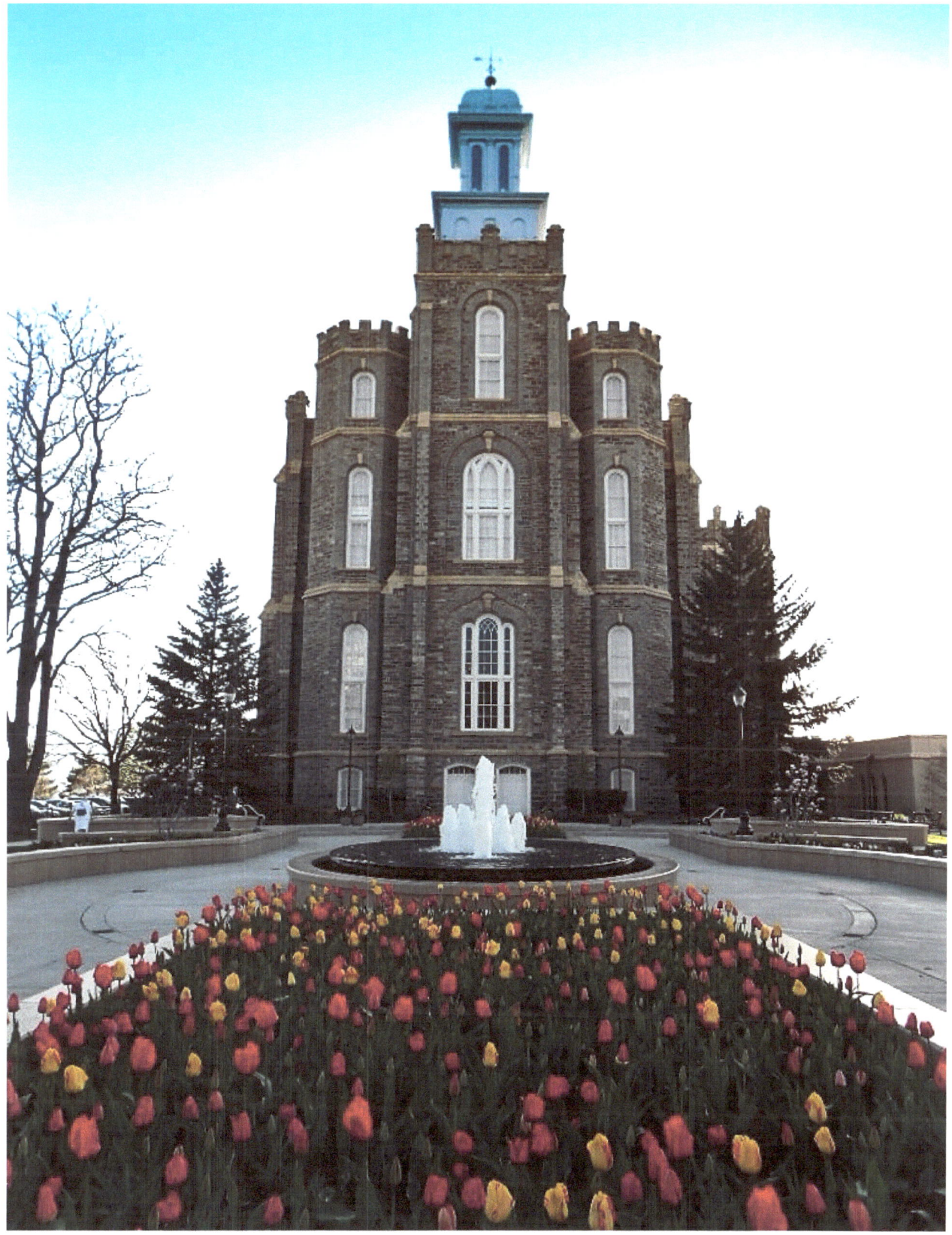

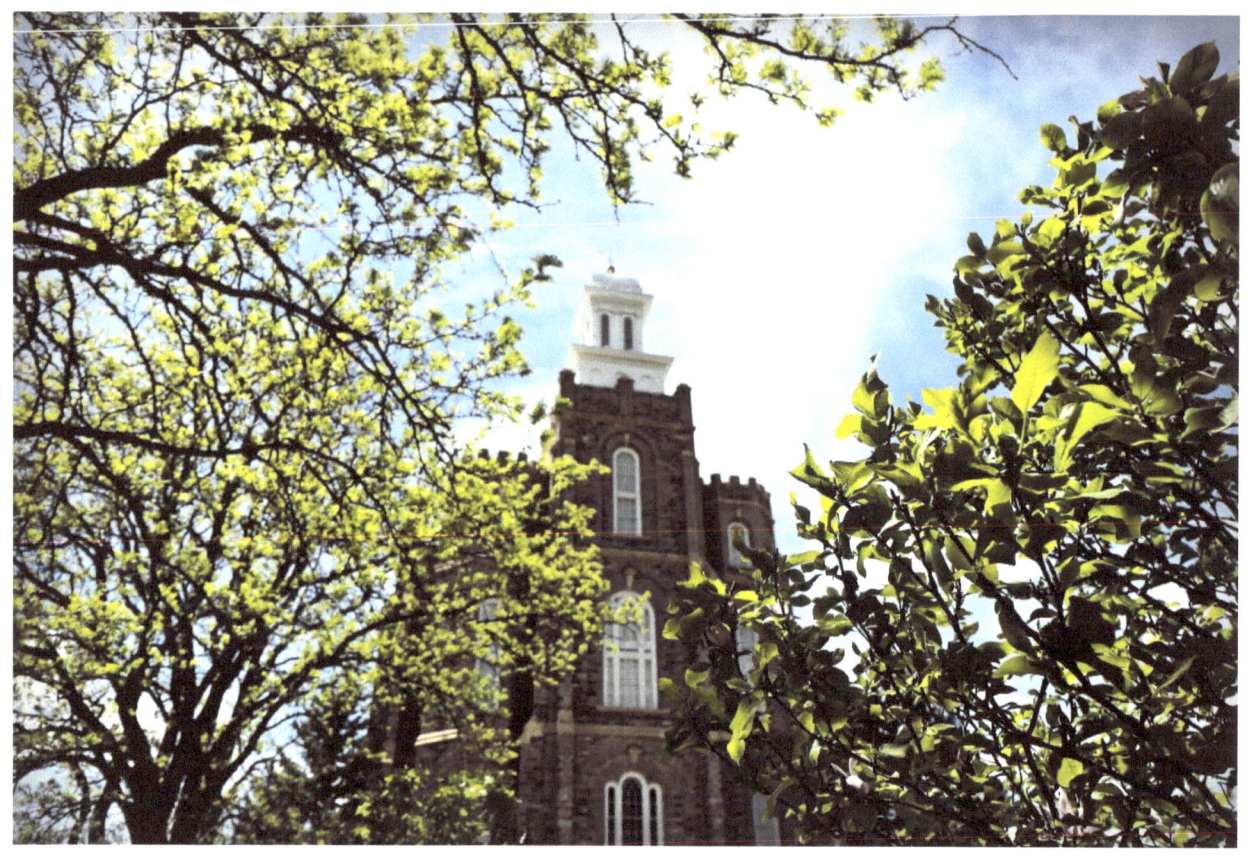

Organize yourselves; prepare every needful thing; and establish a house, even a house of prayer, a house of fasting, a house of faith, a house of learning, a house of glory, a house of order, a house of God;
That your incomings may be in the name of the Lord; that your outgoings may be in the name of the Lord; that all your salutations may be in the name of the Lord, with uplifted hands unto the Most High.

Doctrine & Covenants 88:119-120

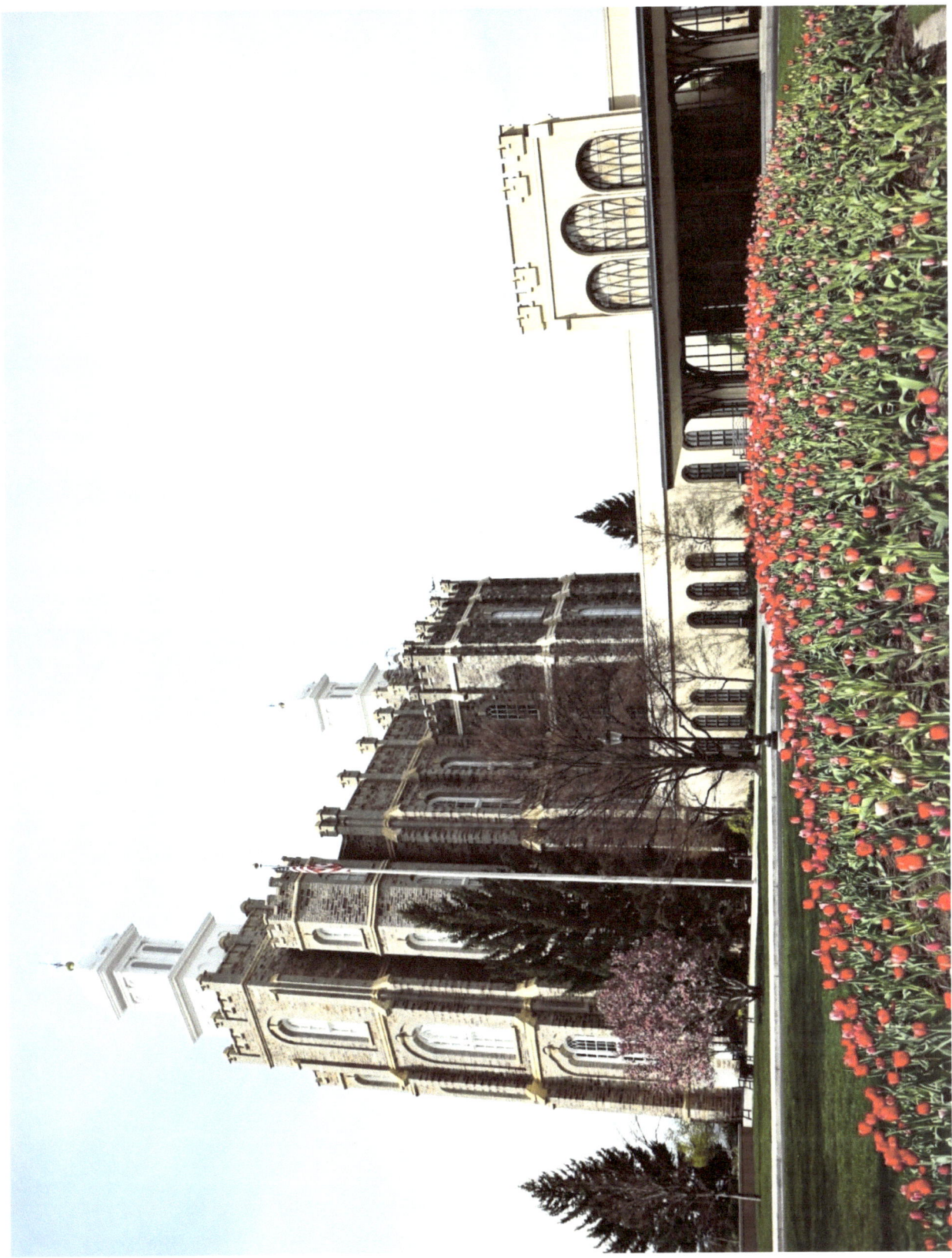

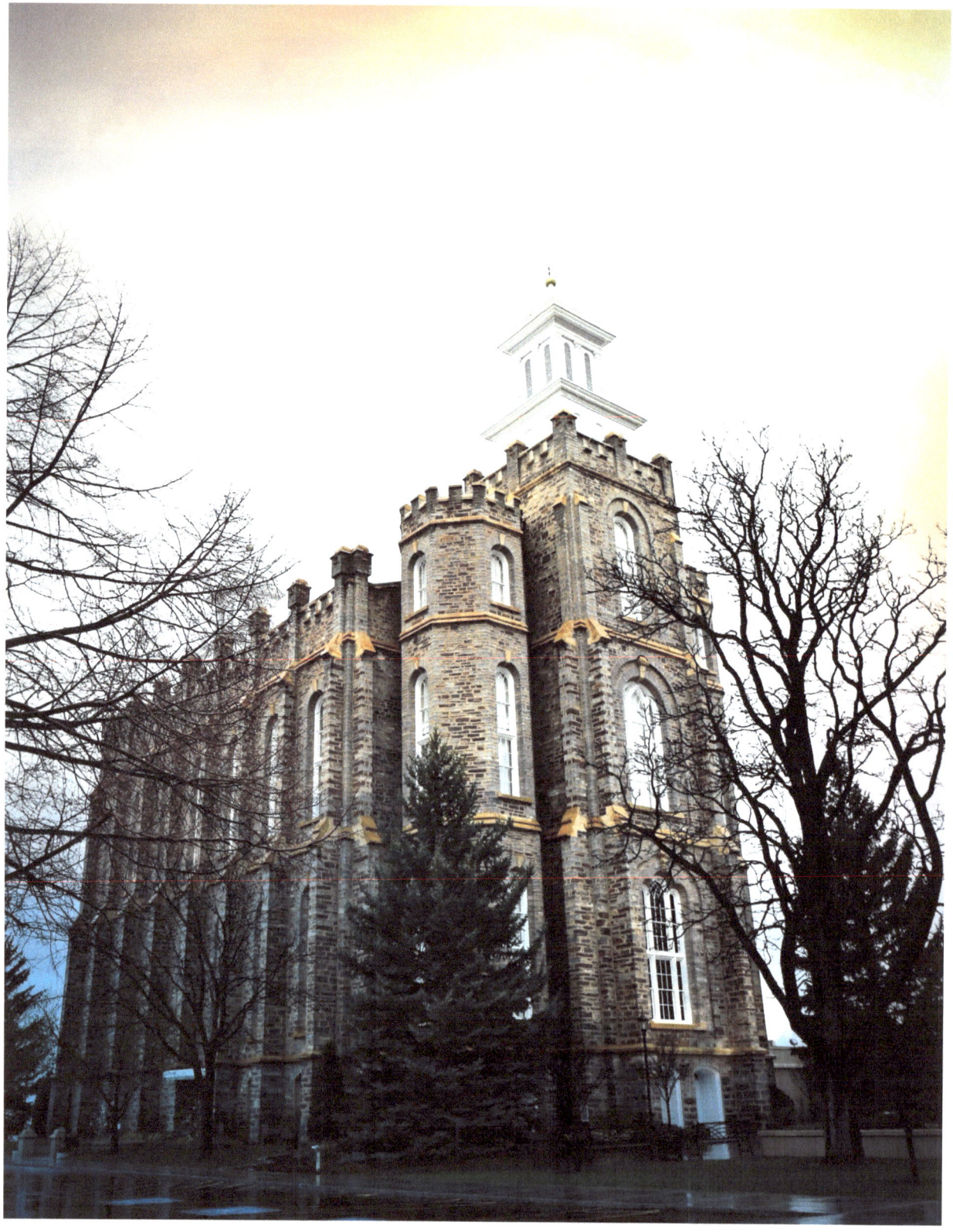

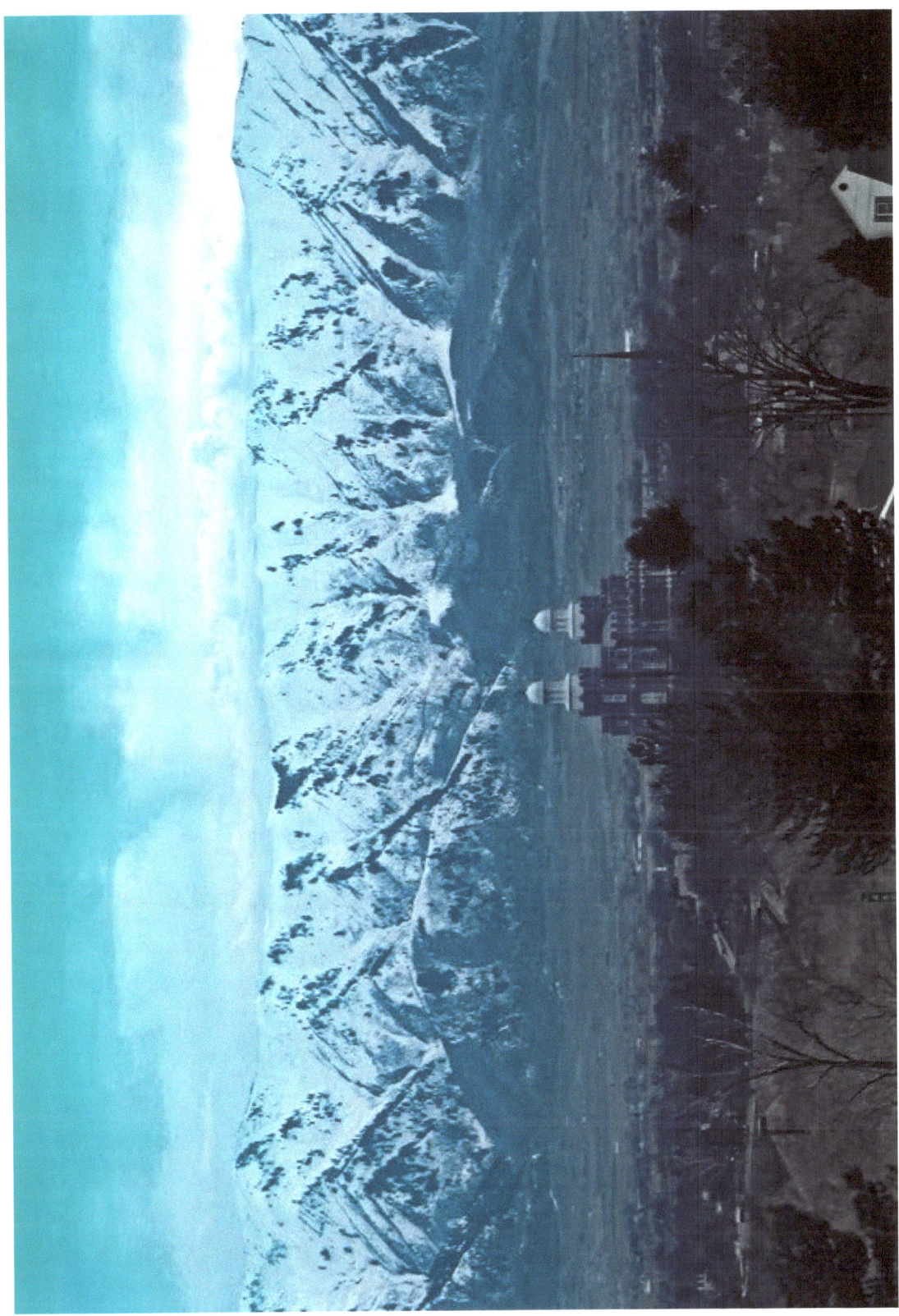

Each of our temples is an expression of our testimony that life beyond the grave is as real and as certain as is our life here on earth. I so testify.

Thomas S. Monson
(The Holy Temple, a Beacon to the World – April 2011)

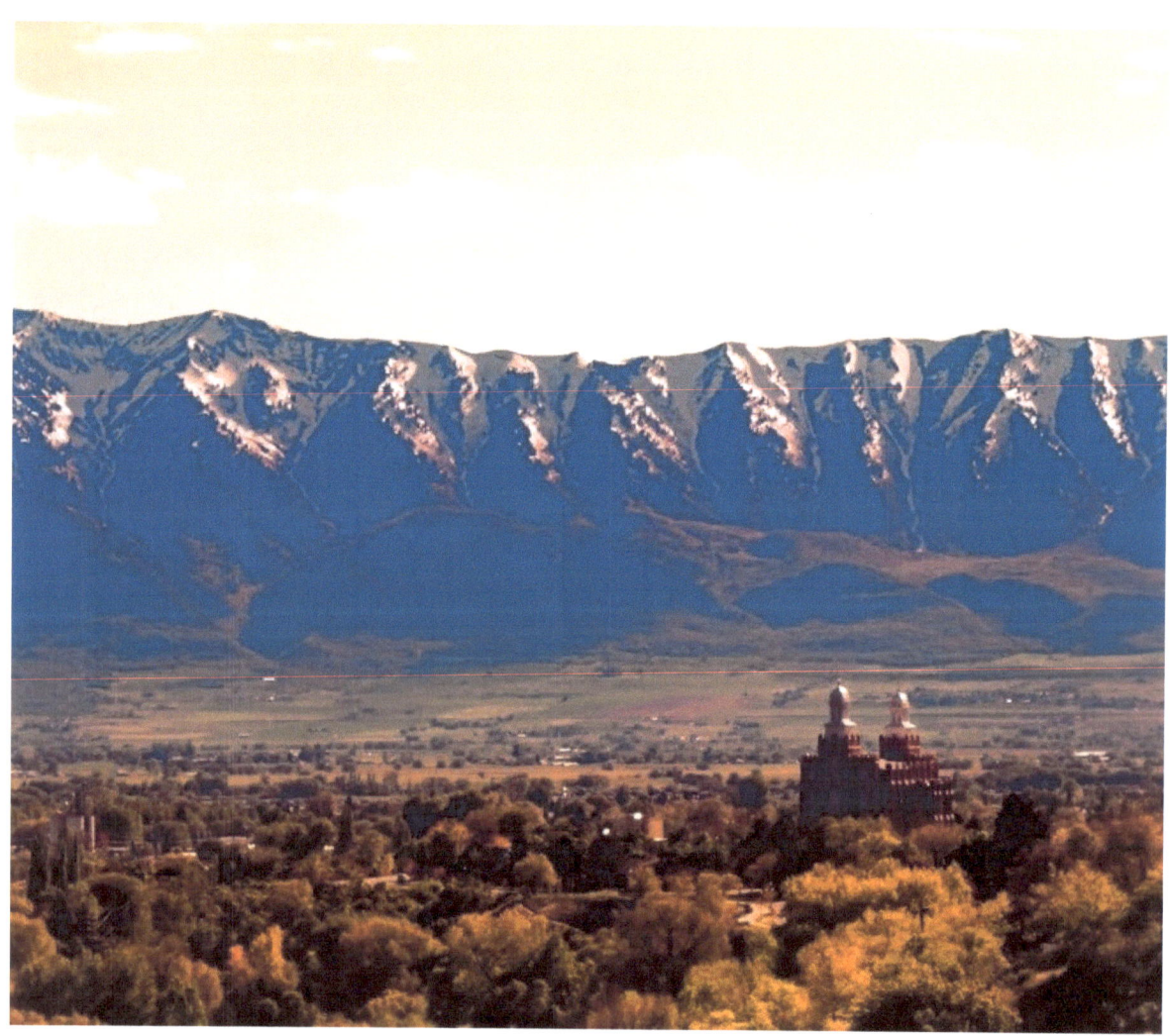

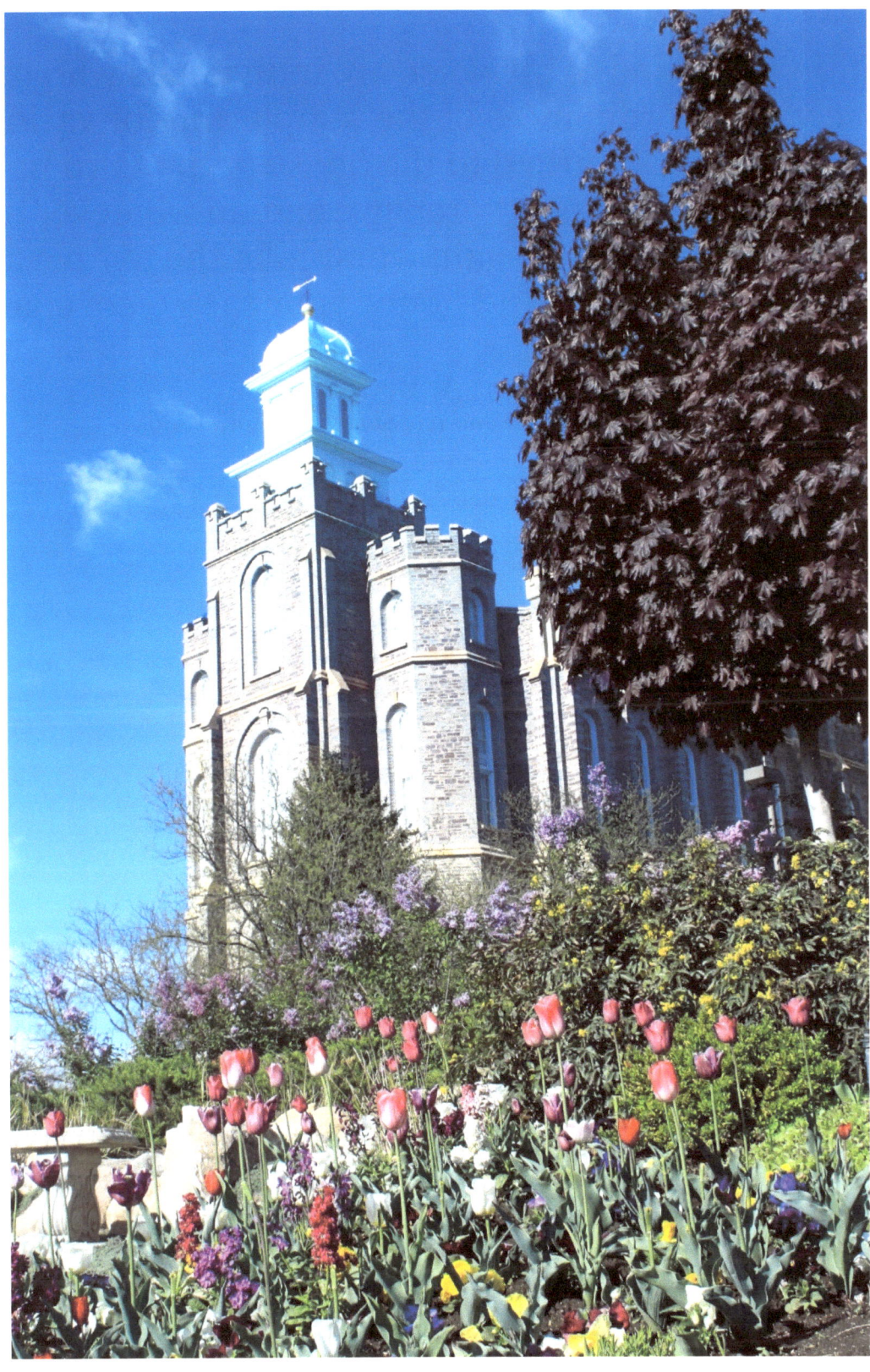

Within the sound of my voice are individuals who have received the ordinances of the temple and for various reasons have not returned to the house of the Lord in quite some time. Please repent, prepare, and do whatever needs to be done so you can again worship in the temple and more fully remember and honor your sacred covenants.

David A. Bednar
(Honorably Hold a Name and Standing – April 2009)

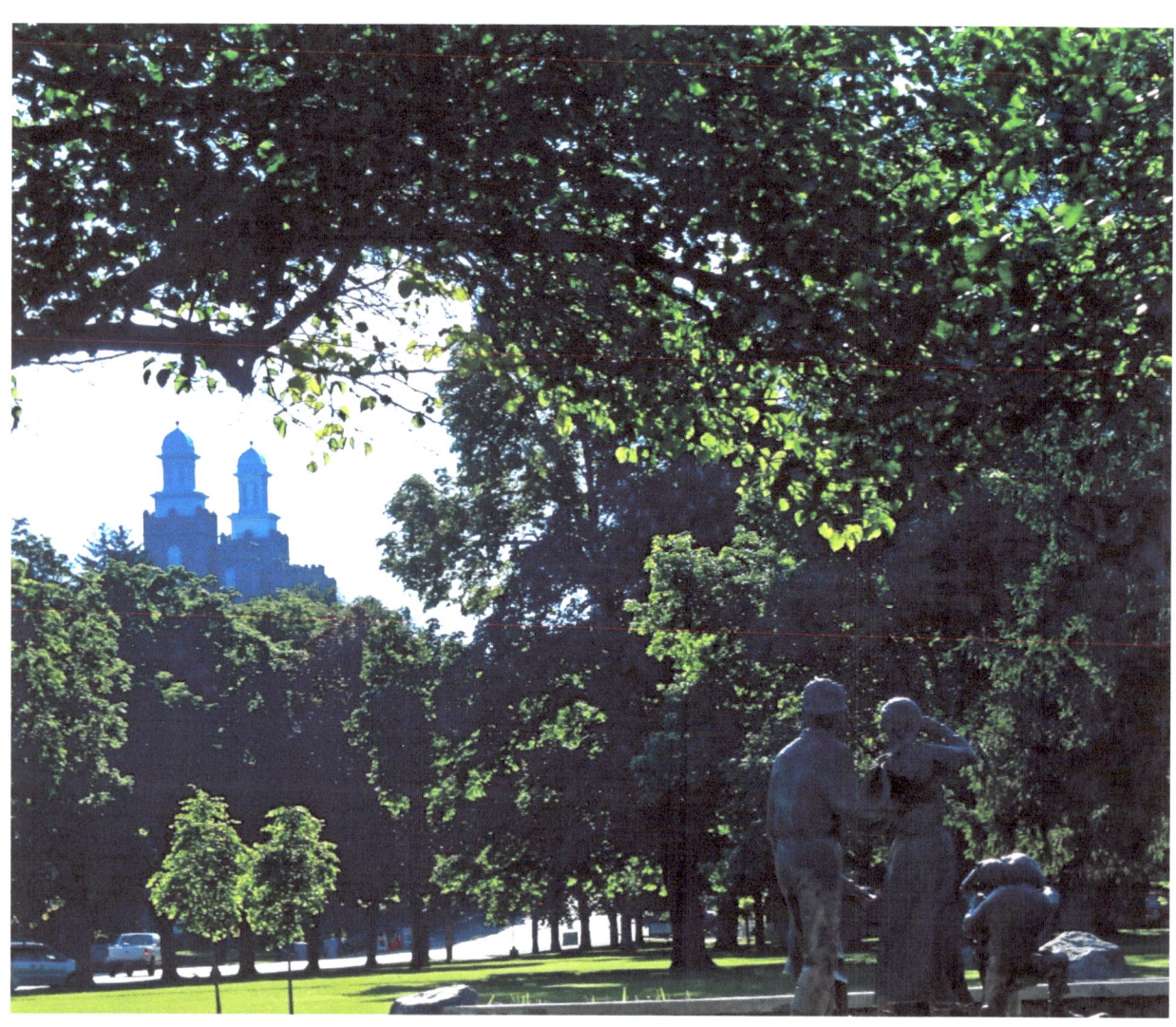

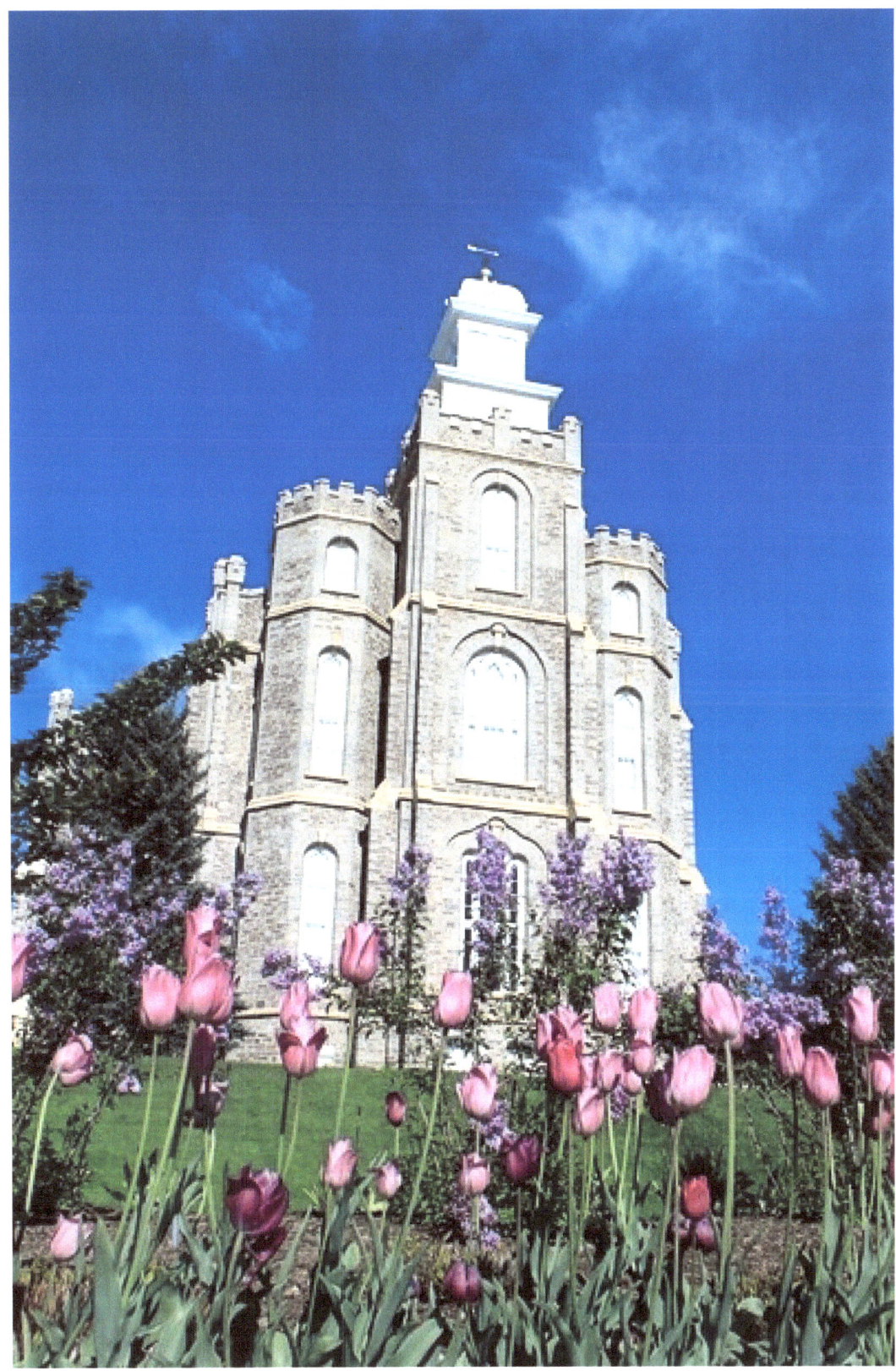

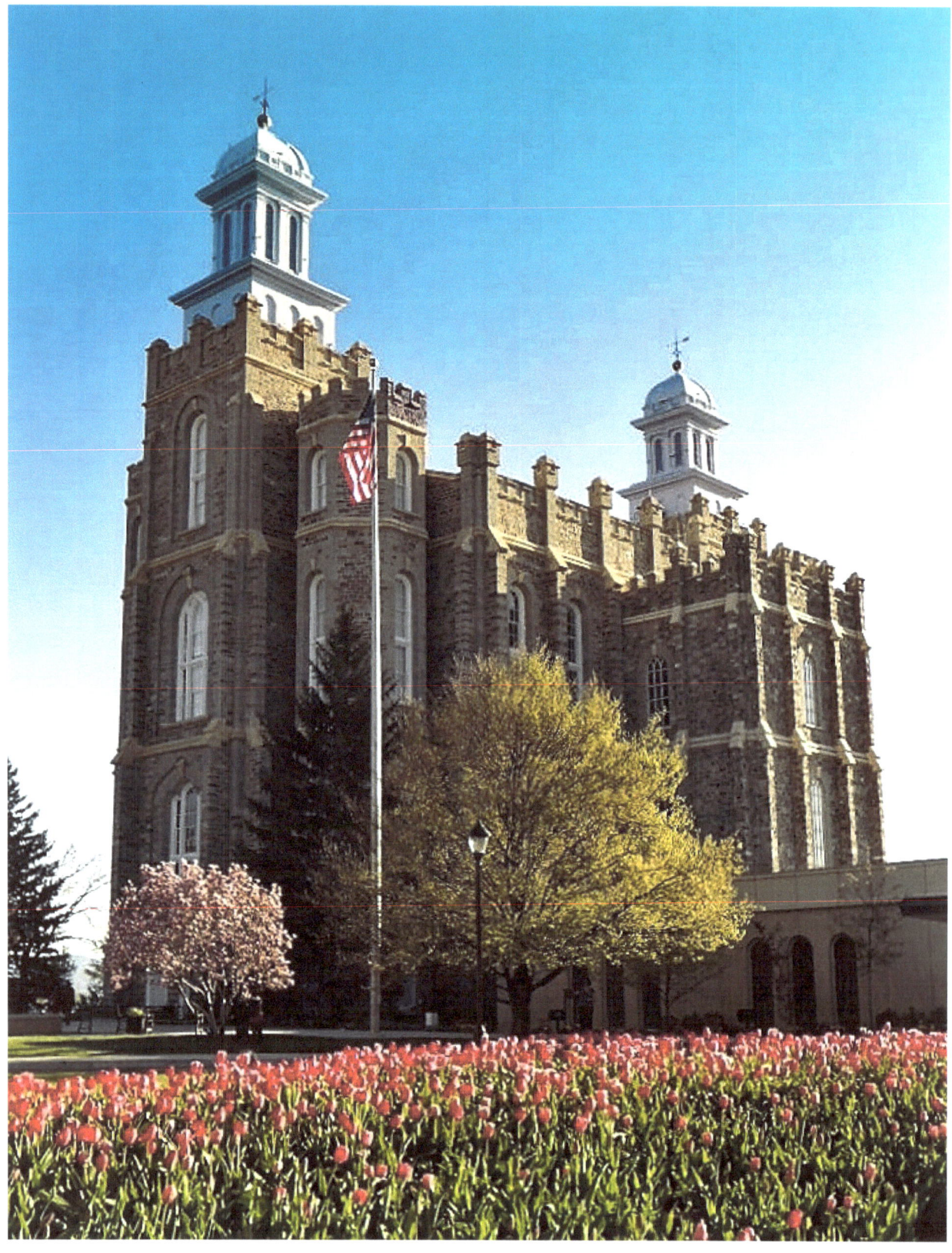

Hear, all ye people; hearken, O earth, and all that therein is: and let the Lord God be witness against you, the Lord from his holy temple.

Micah 1:2

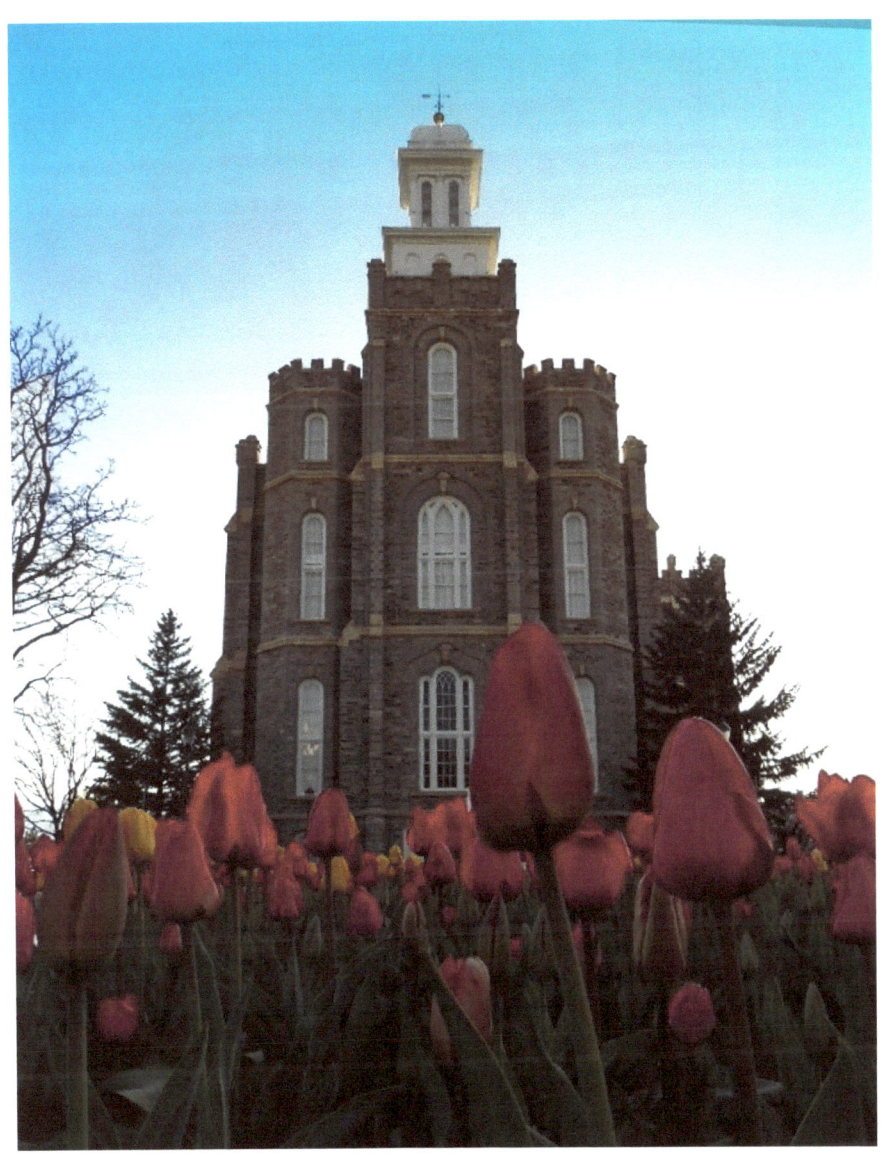

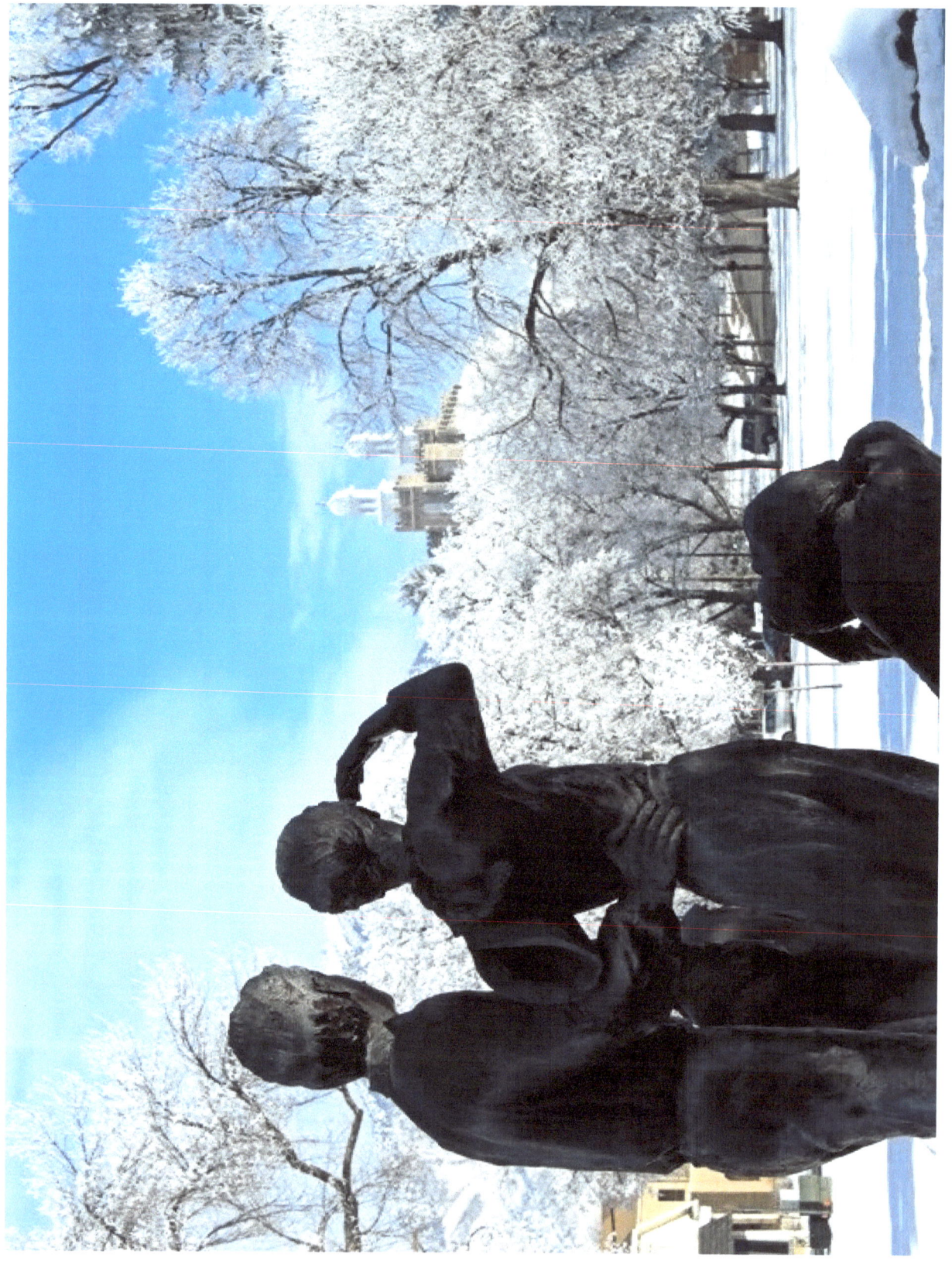

And the temple of God was opened in heaven, and there
was seen in his temple the ark of his testament:
and there were lightnings, and voices, and thunderings,
and an earthquake, and great hail.

Revelation 1:19

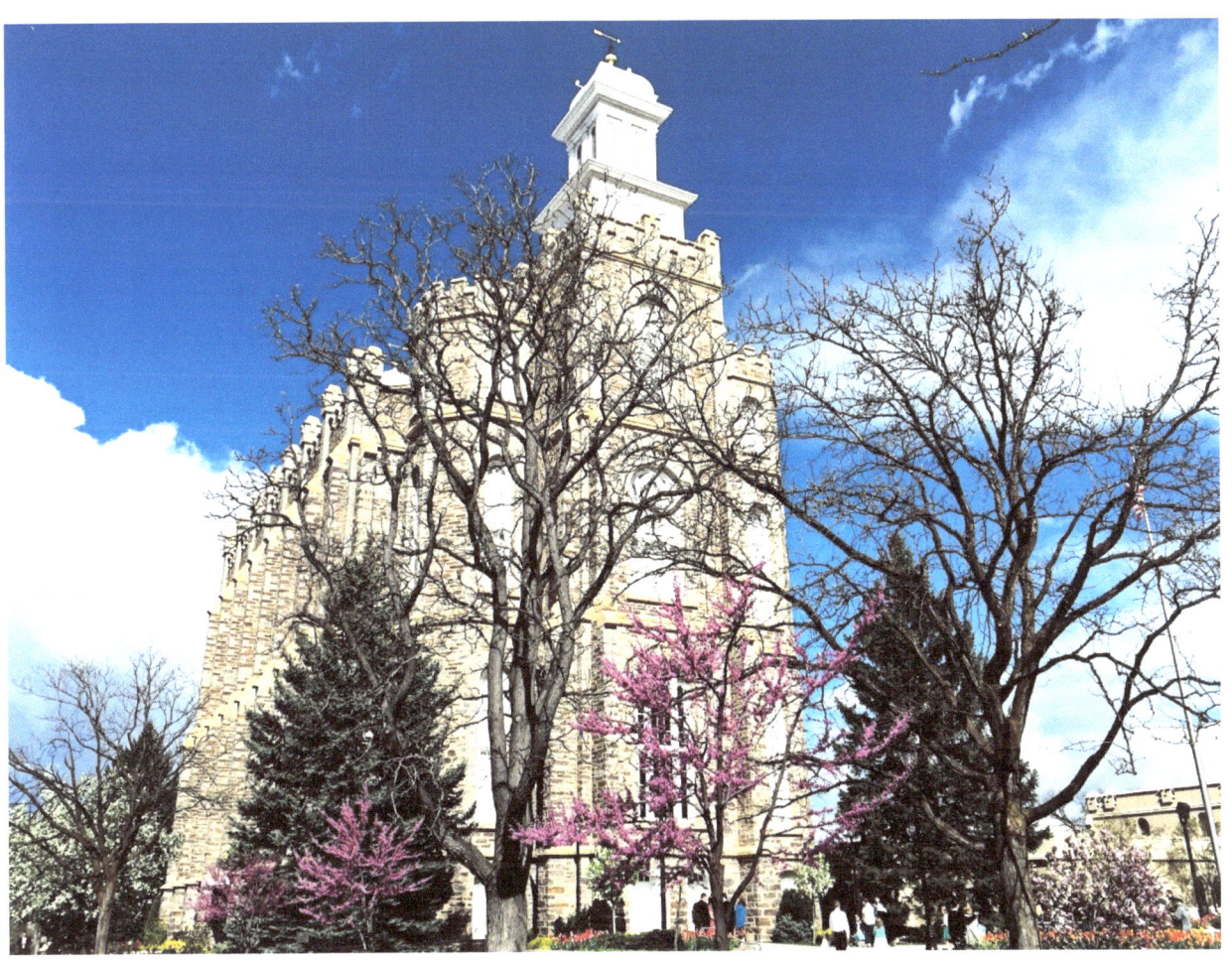

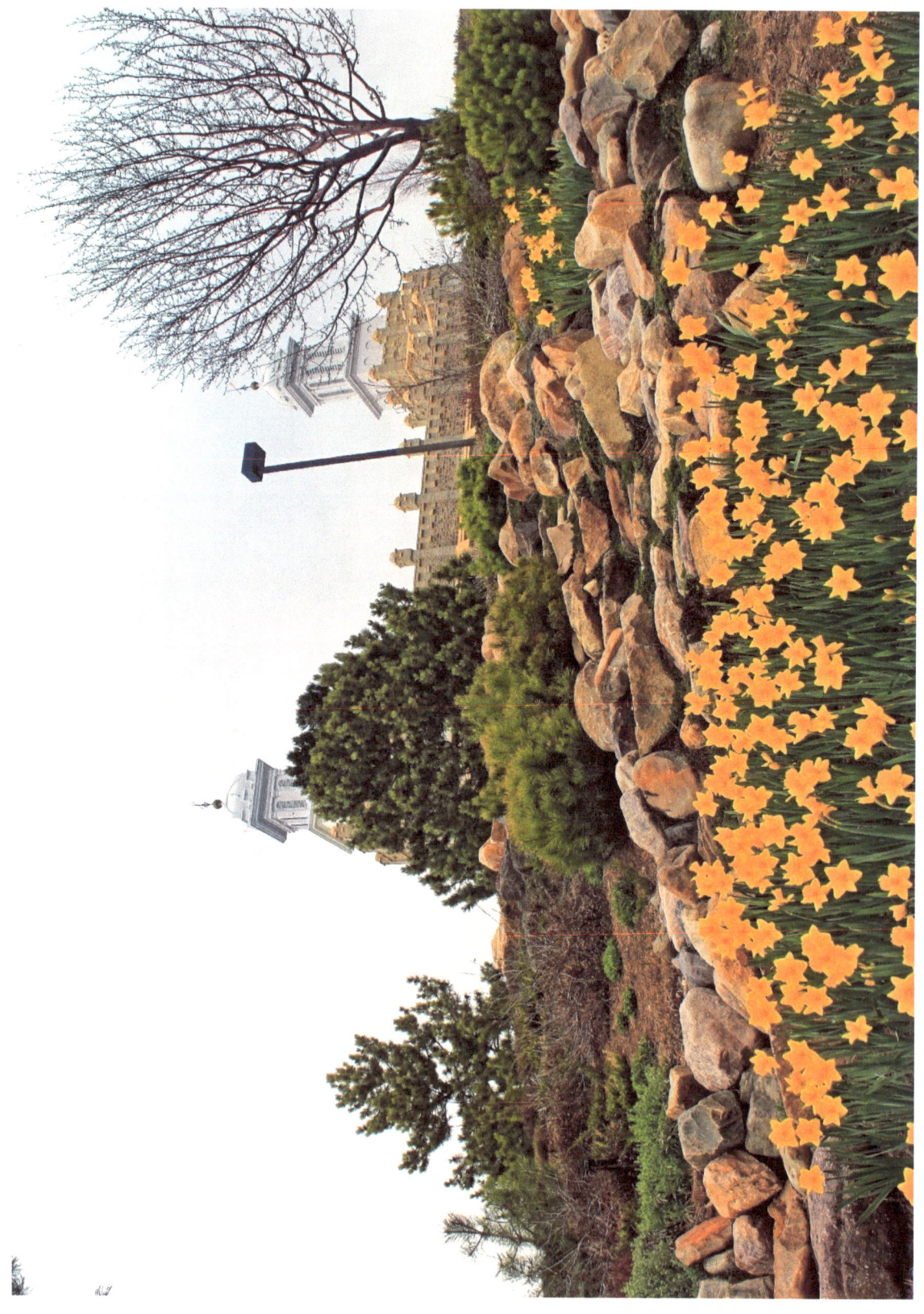

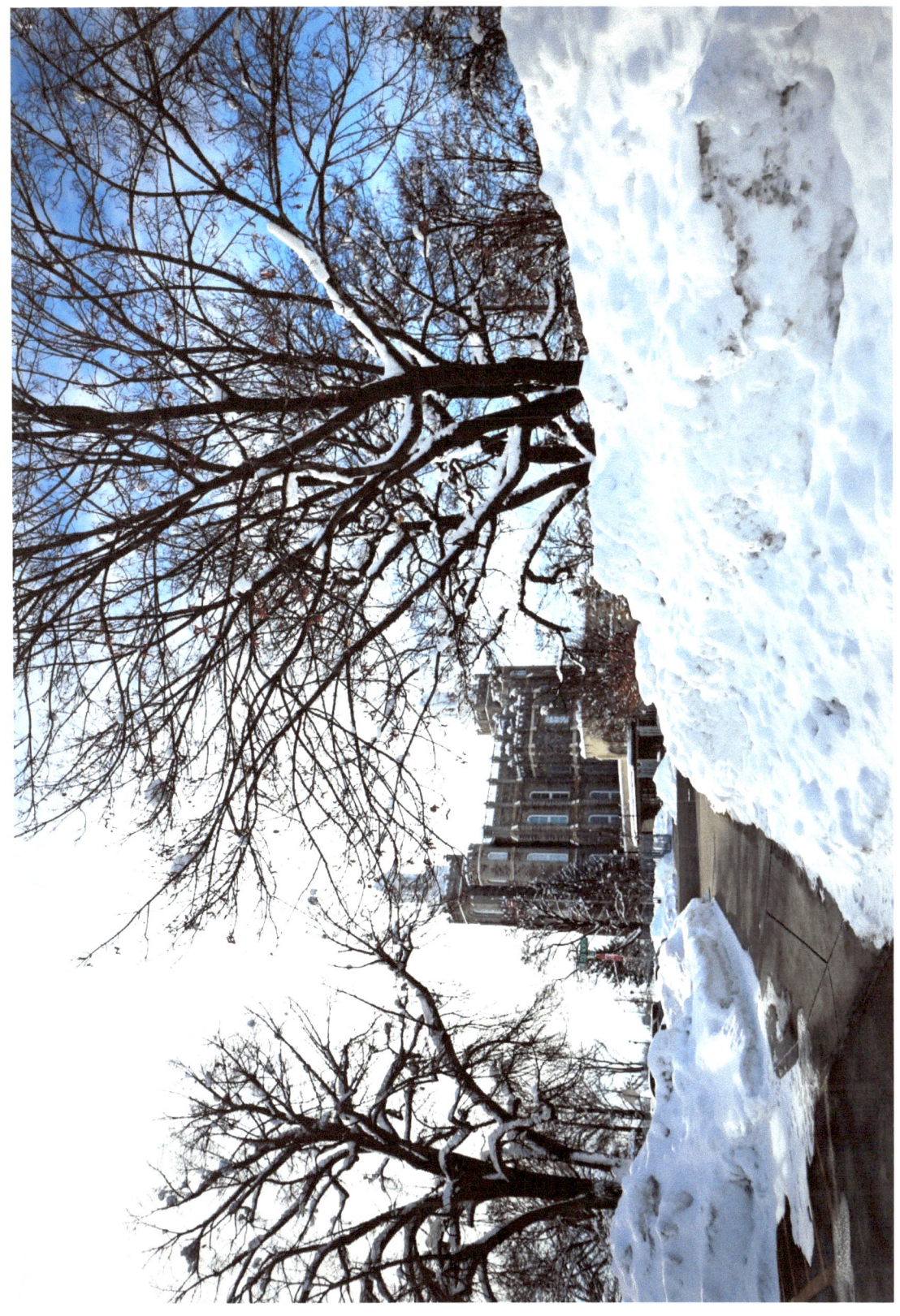

Speak unto all the congregation of the children of Israel,
and say unto them, Ye shall be holy:
for I the Lord your God am holy.

Leviticus 19:2

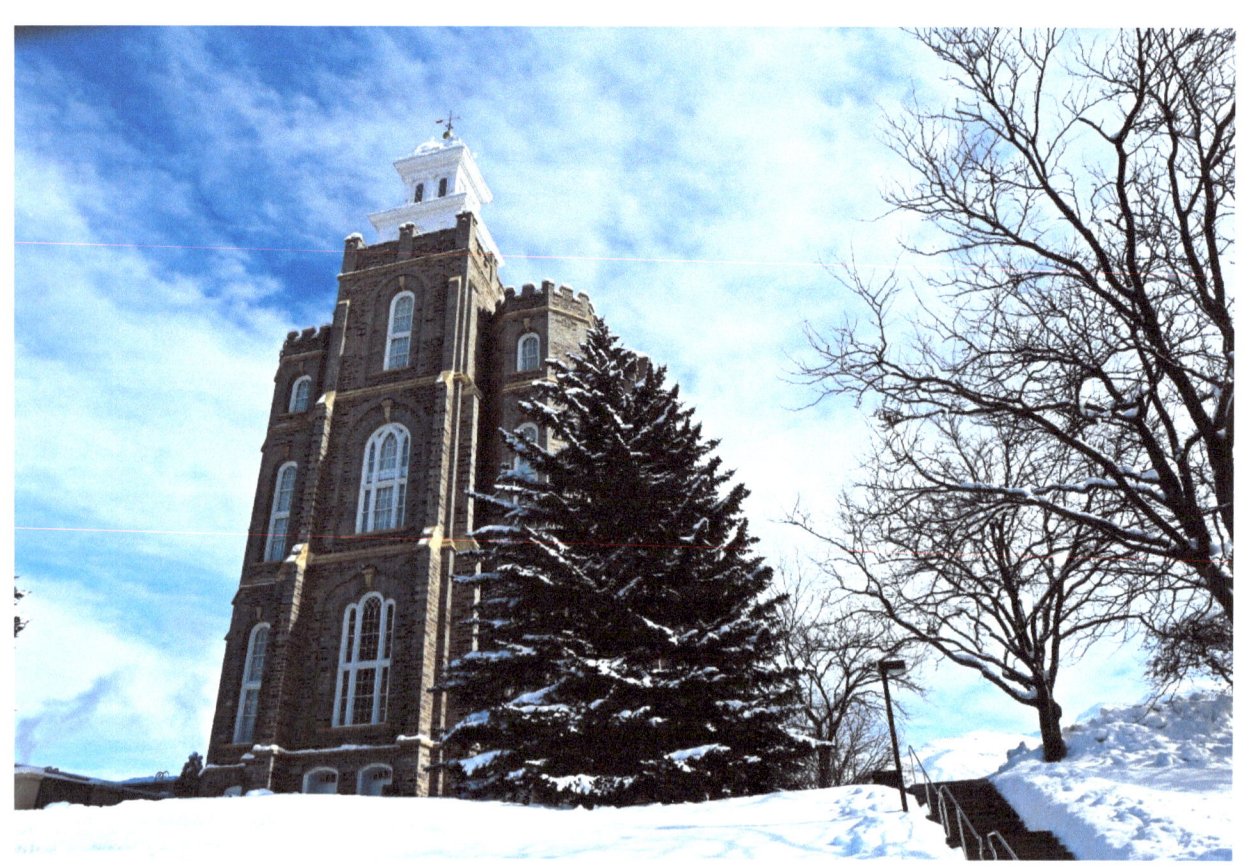

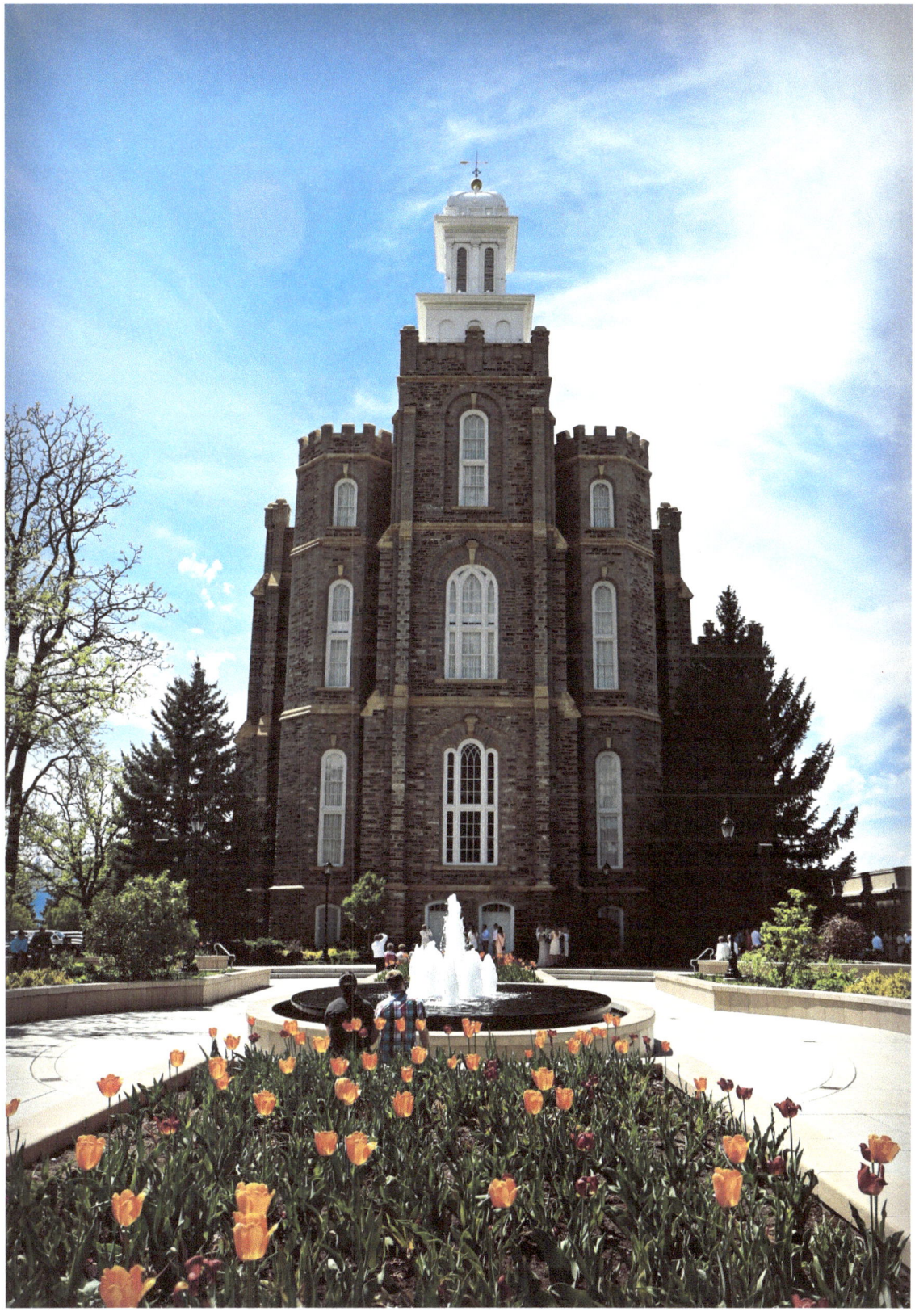

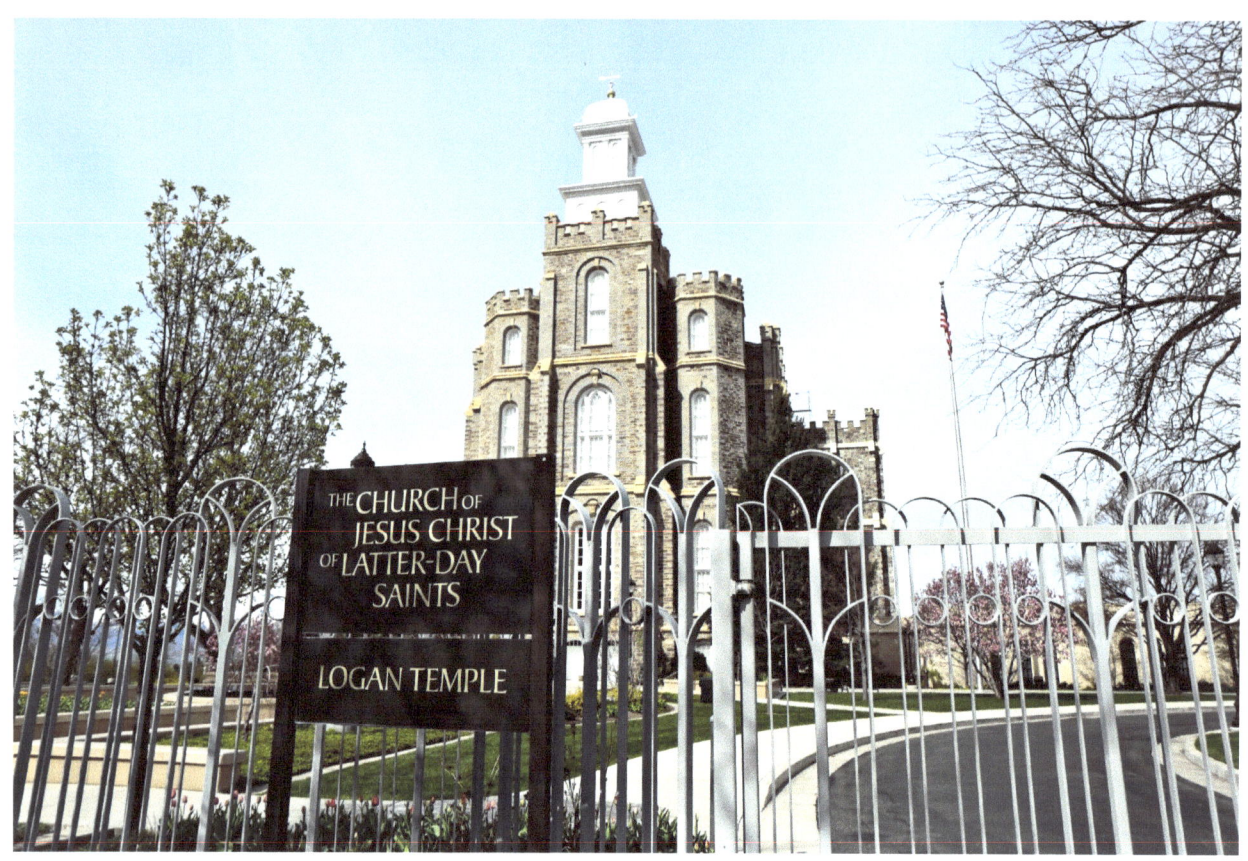

As we touch the temple and love the temple, our lives will
reflect our faith. As we go to the holy house,
as we remember the covenants we make therein,
we will be able to bear every trial
and overcome each temptation.

Thomas S. Monson
(Blessings of the Temple, Liahona October 2010)

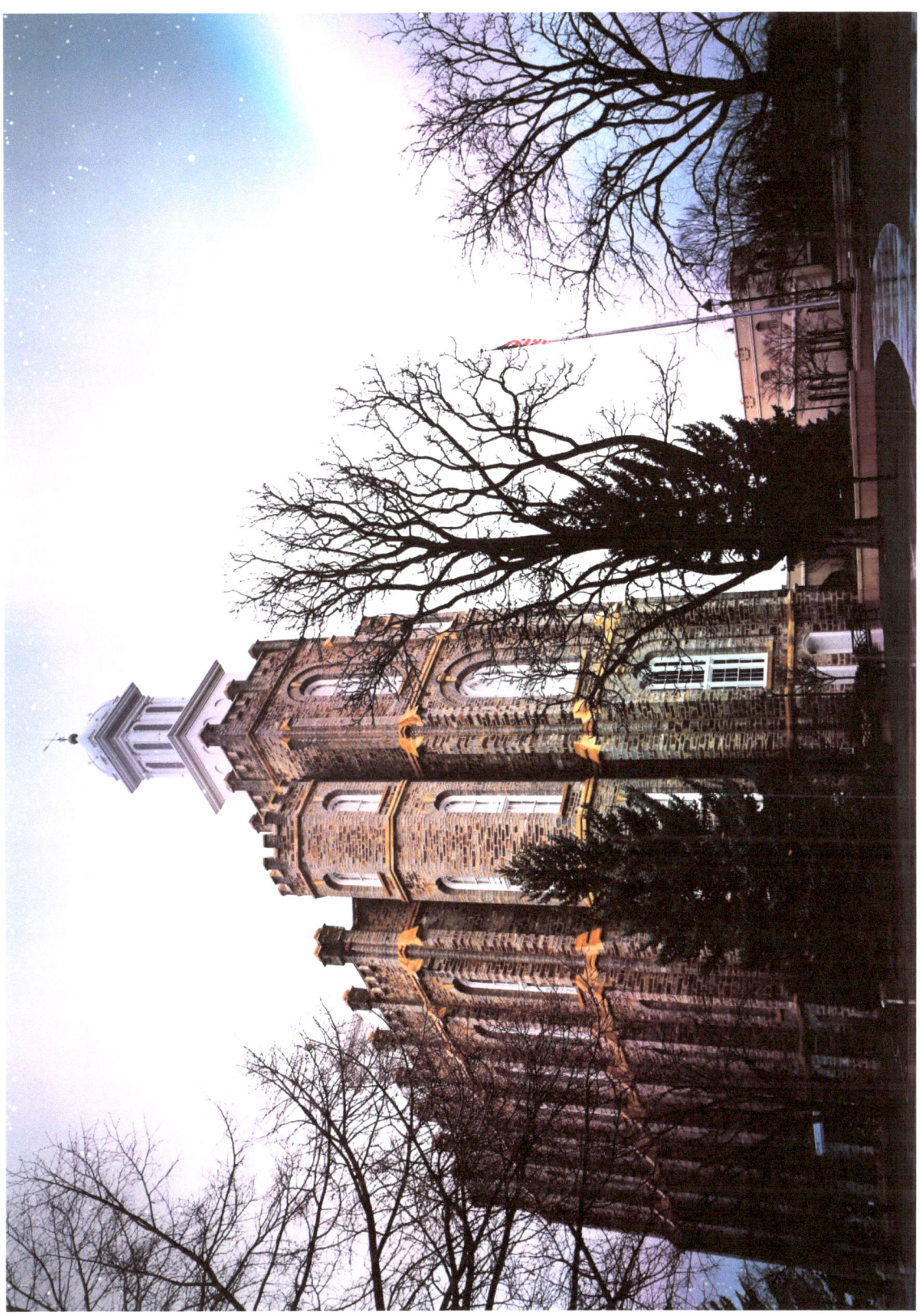

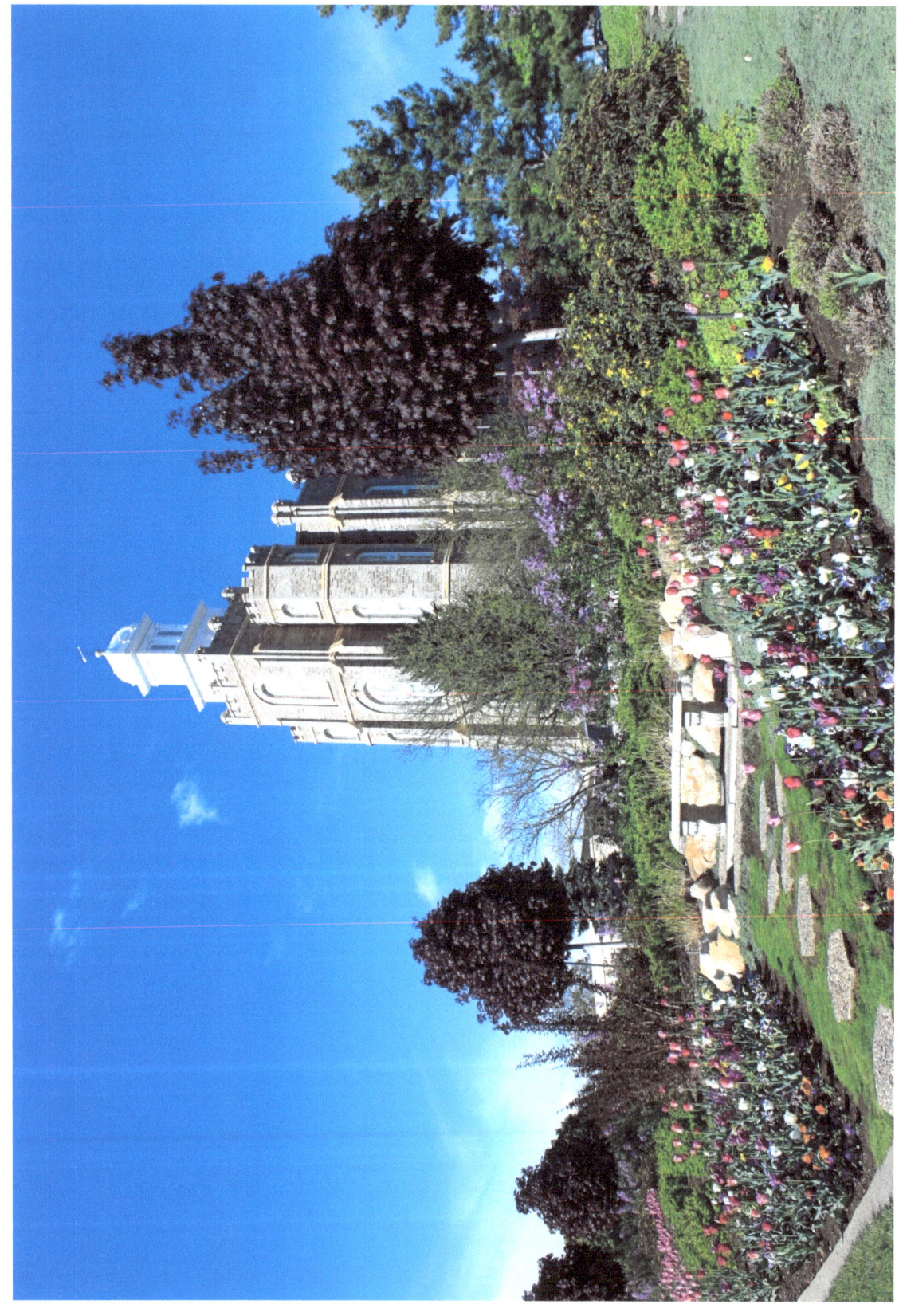

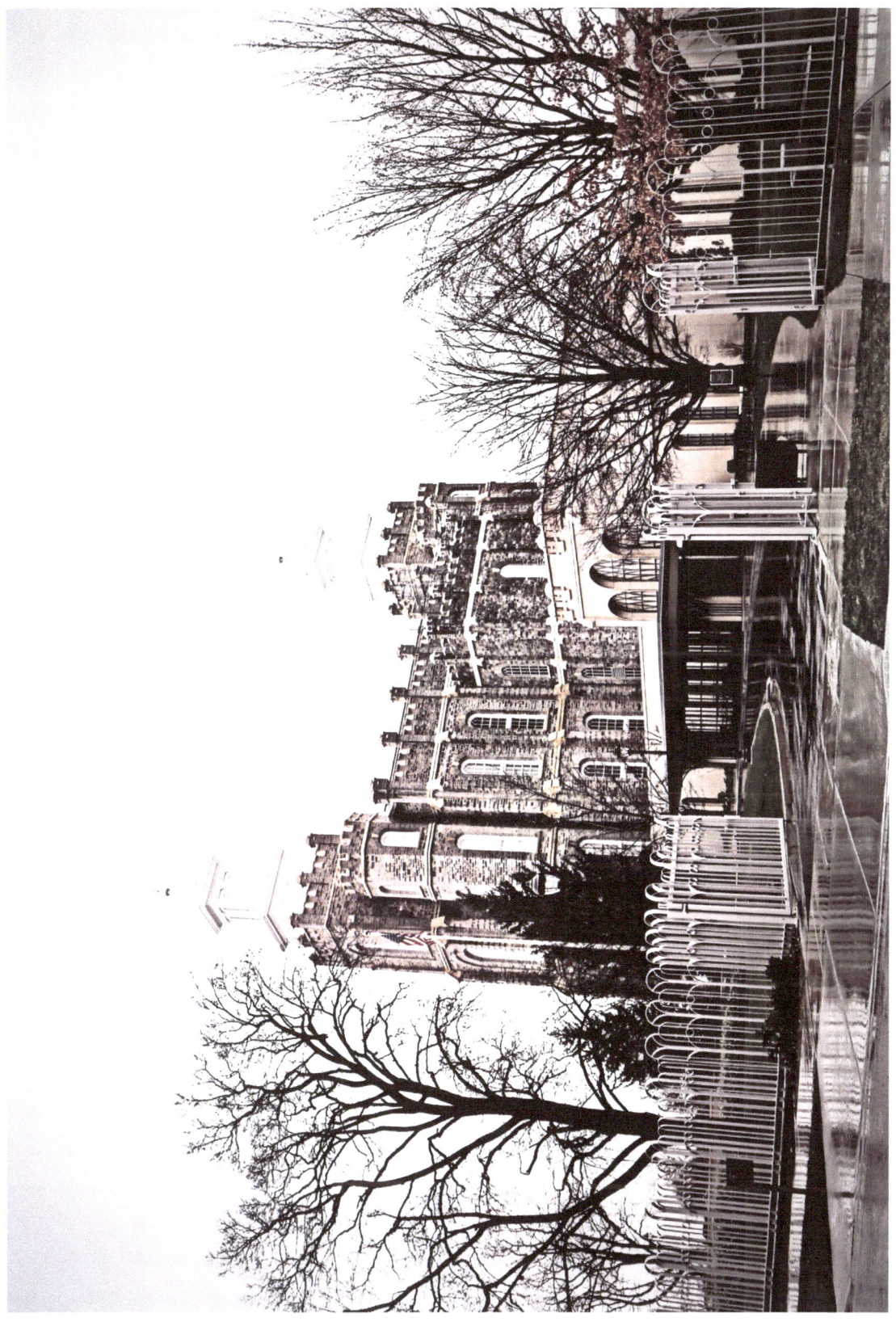

If any man defile the temple of God,
him shall God destroy; for the temple of God is holy,
which temple ye are.

I Corinthians 3:17

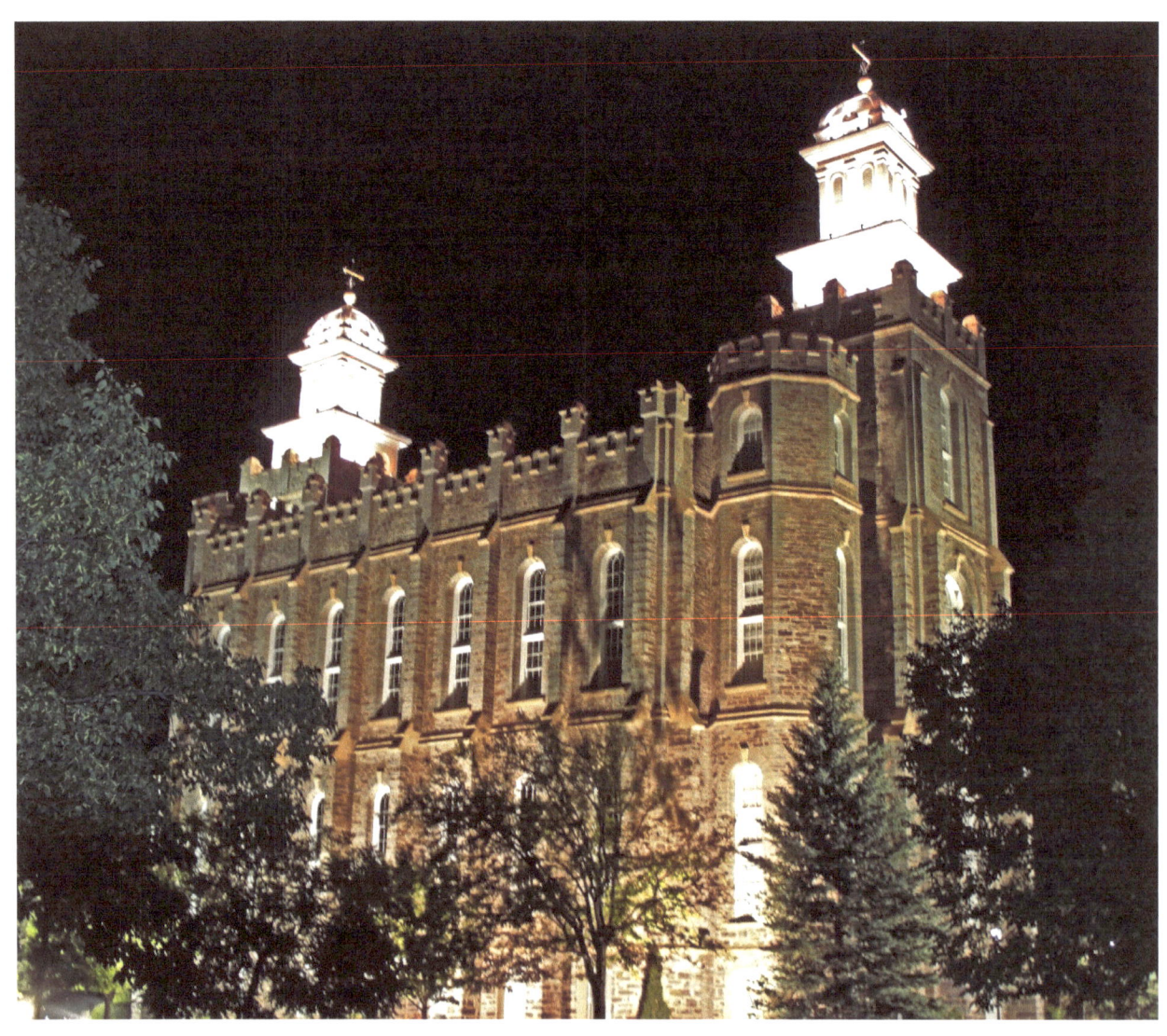

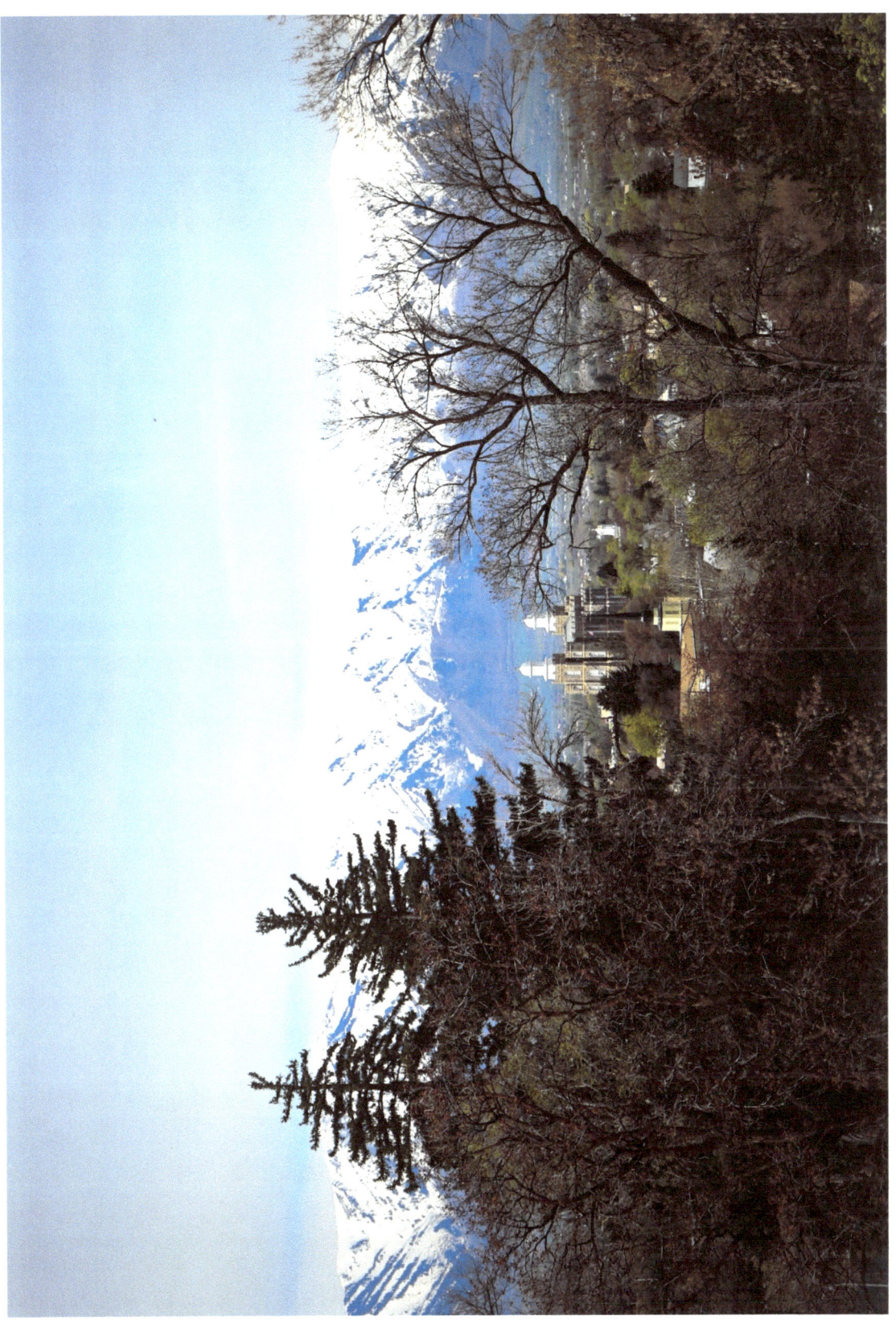

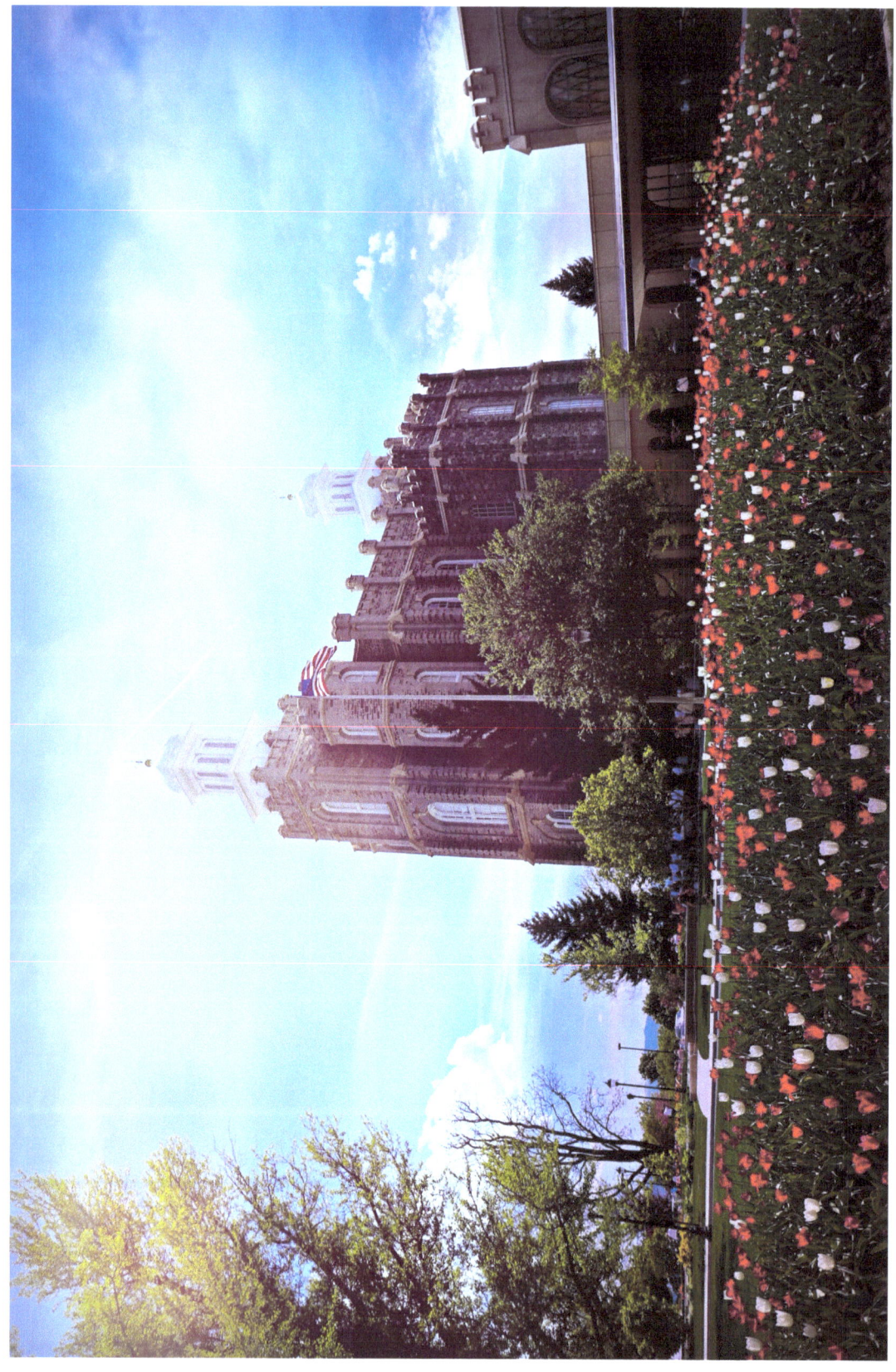

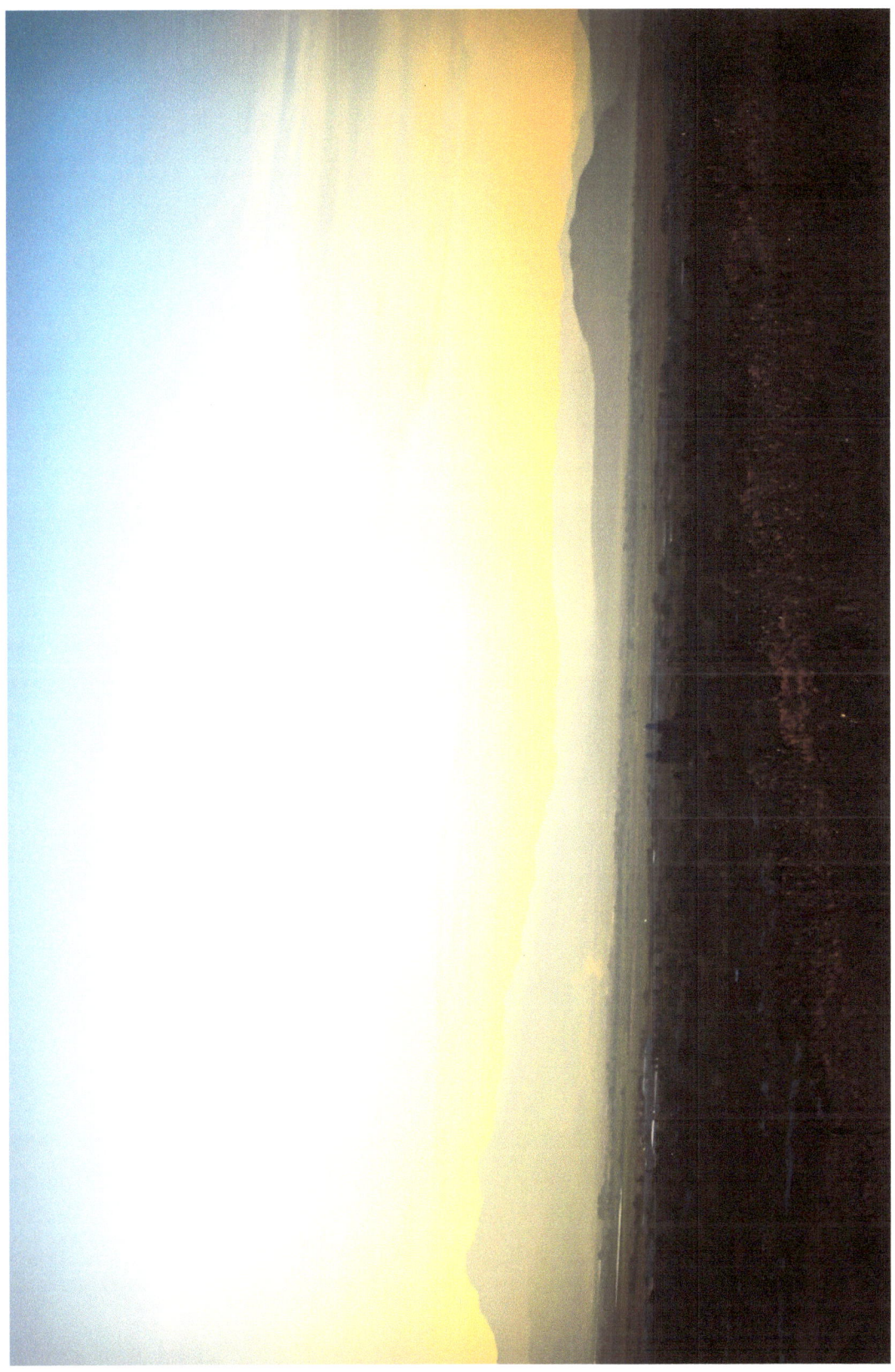

You are never lost when you can see the temple. The temple will provide direction for you and your family in a world filled with chaos. It is an eternal guidepost which will help you from getting lost in the 'mist of darkness.

Gary E. Stevenson
(Sacred Homes, Sacred Temples, April 2009)

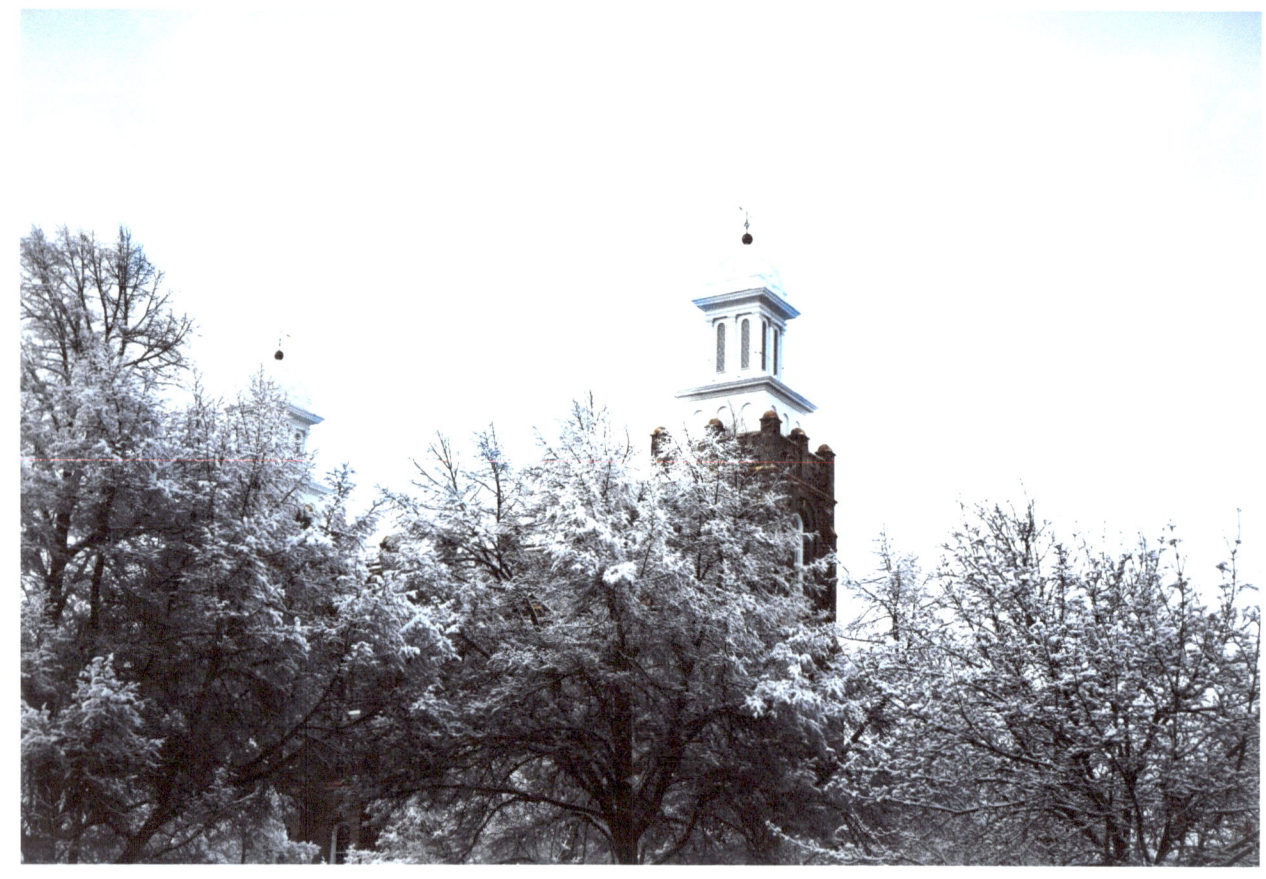

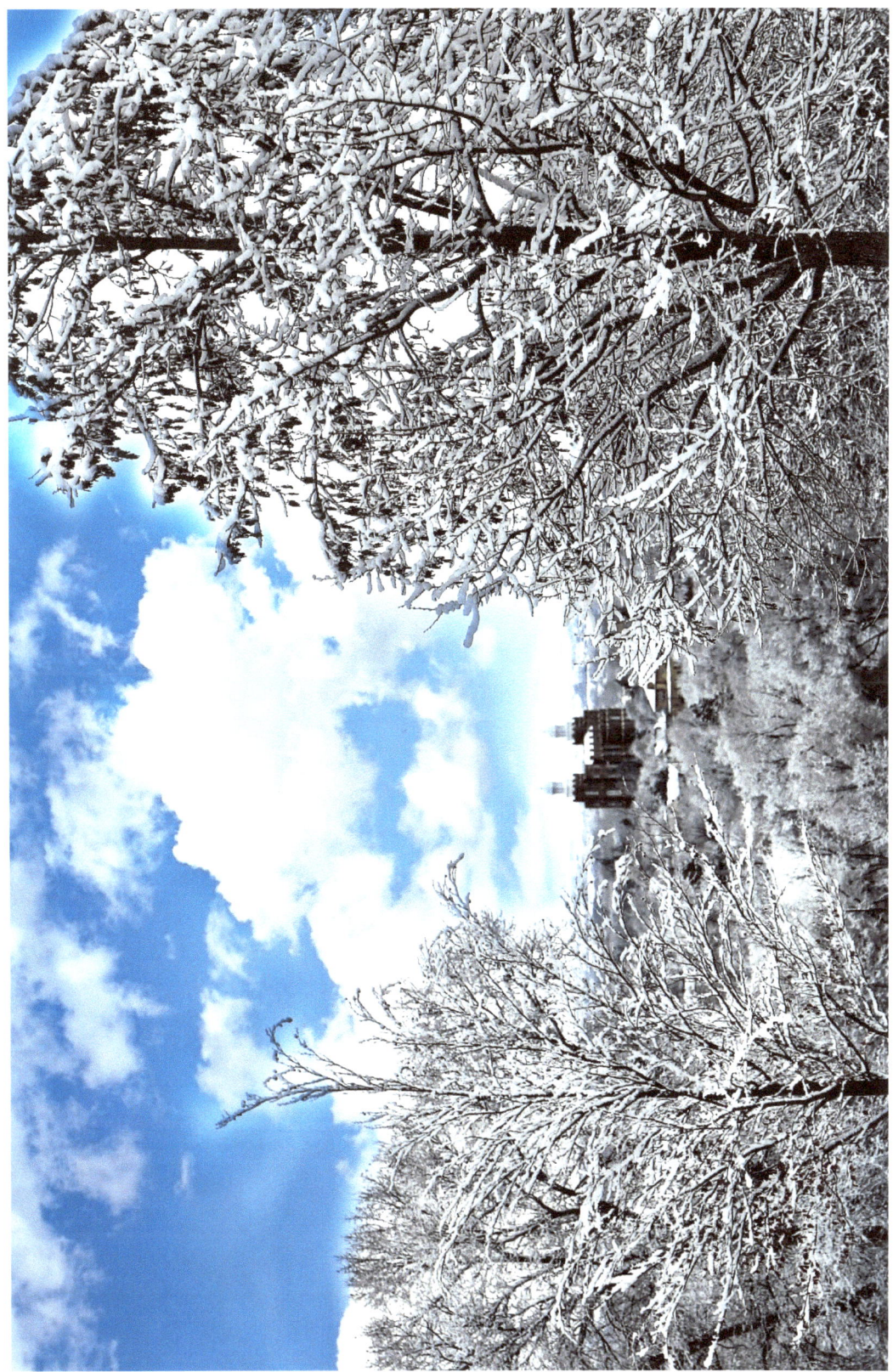

I am Jesus Christ, the Son of God; wherefore, gird up your loins and I will suddenly come to my temple. Even so. Amen.

Doctrine & Covenants 36:8

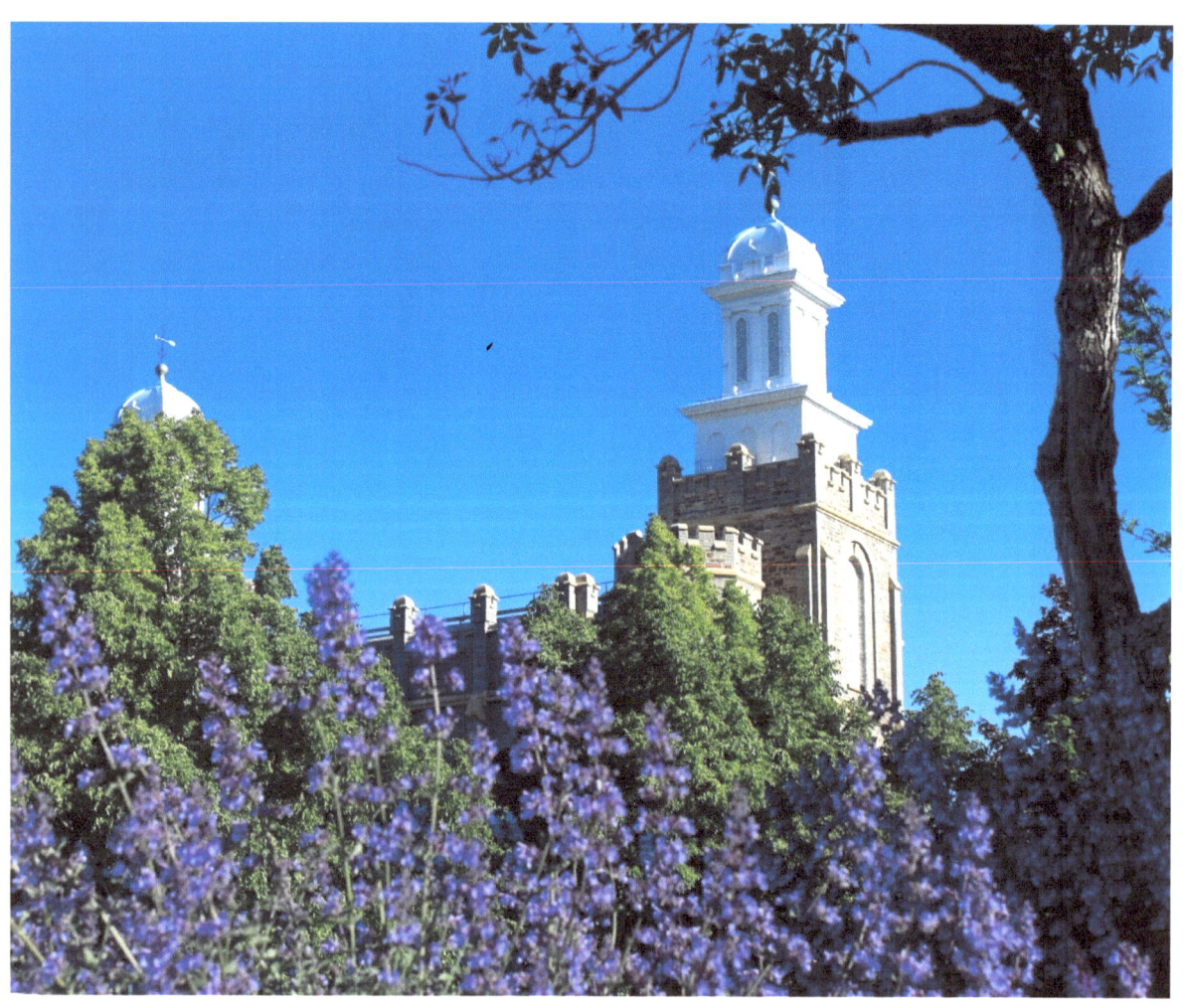

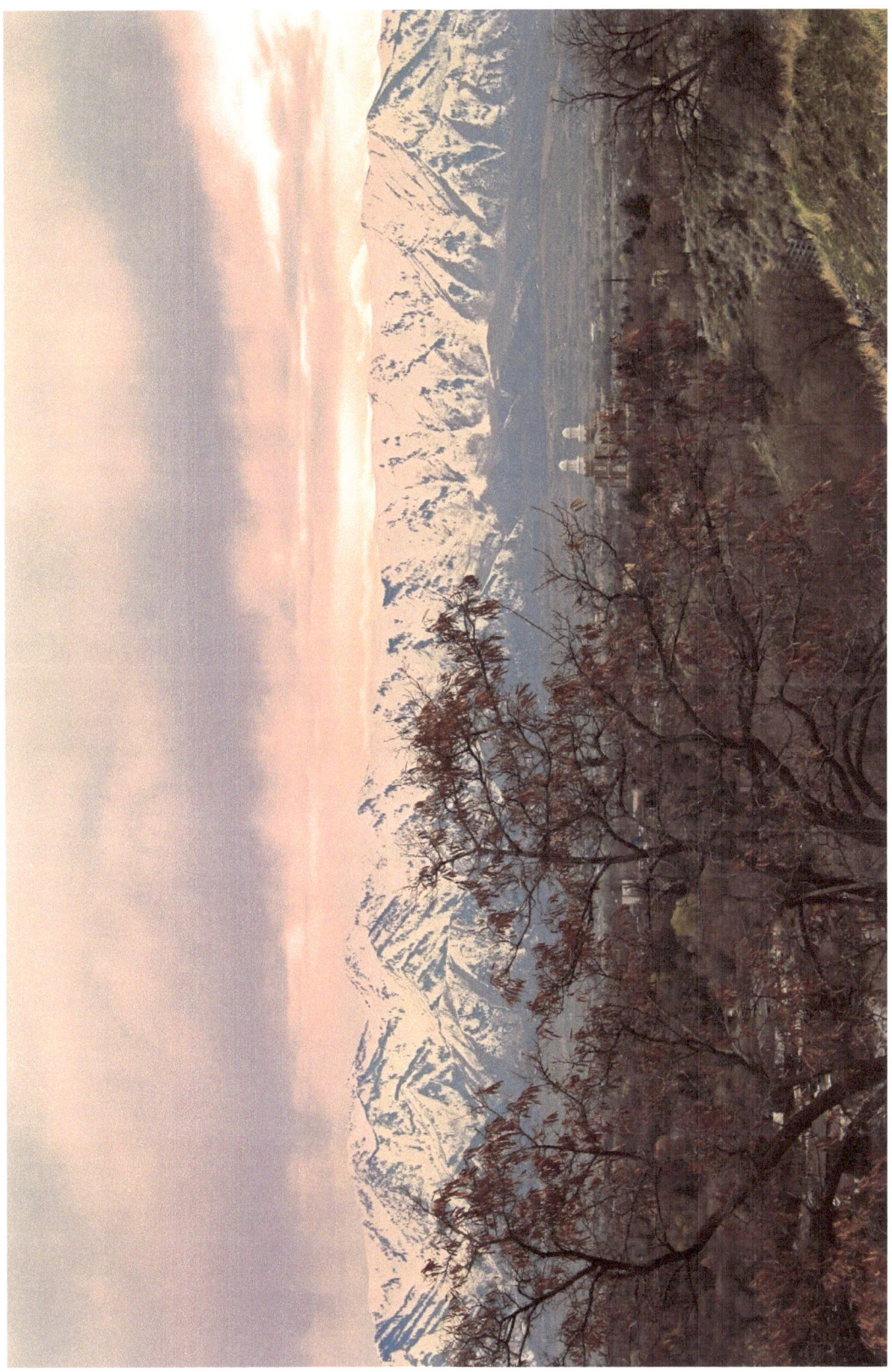

Each holy temple stands as a symbol of our membership in the Church, as a sign of our faith in life after death, and as a sacred step toward eternal glory for us and our families.

Russell M. Nelson
(Personal Preparation for Temple Blessings, April 2001)

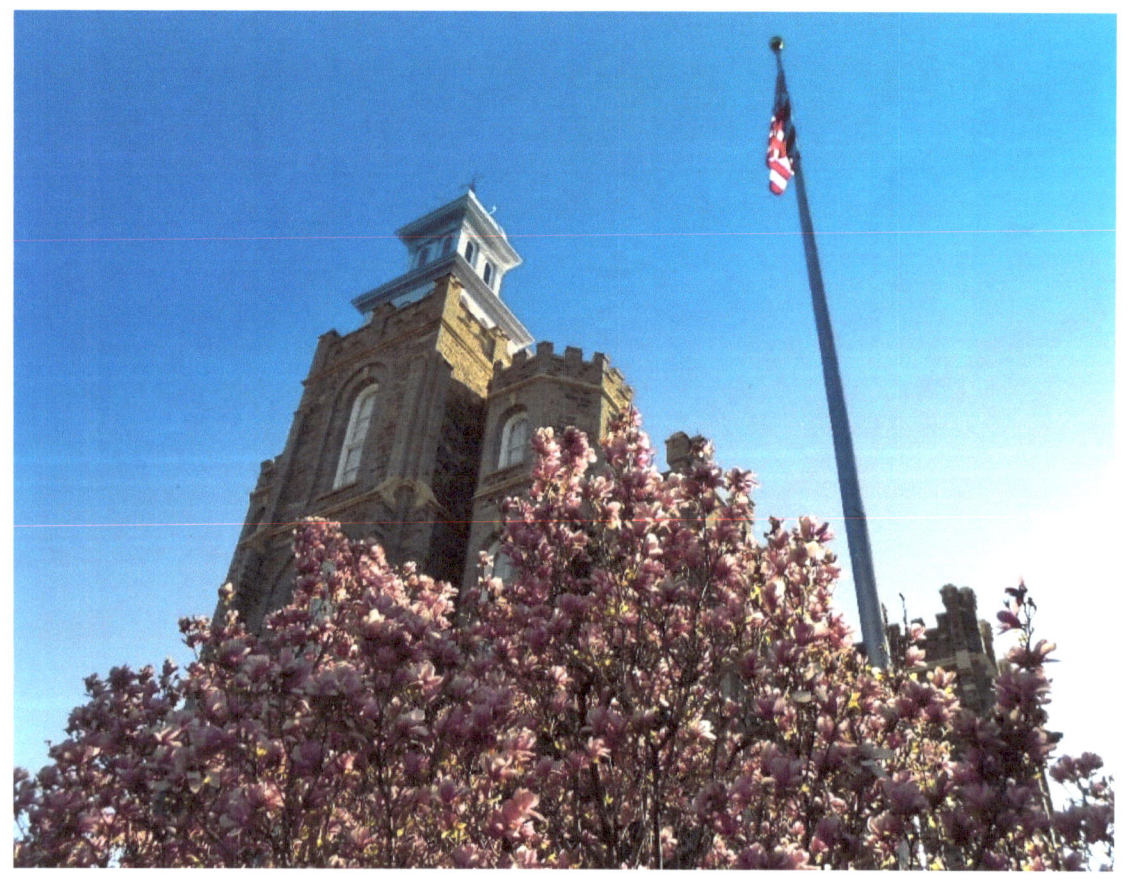

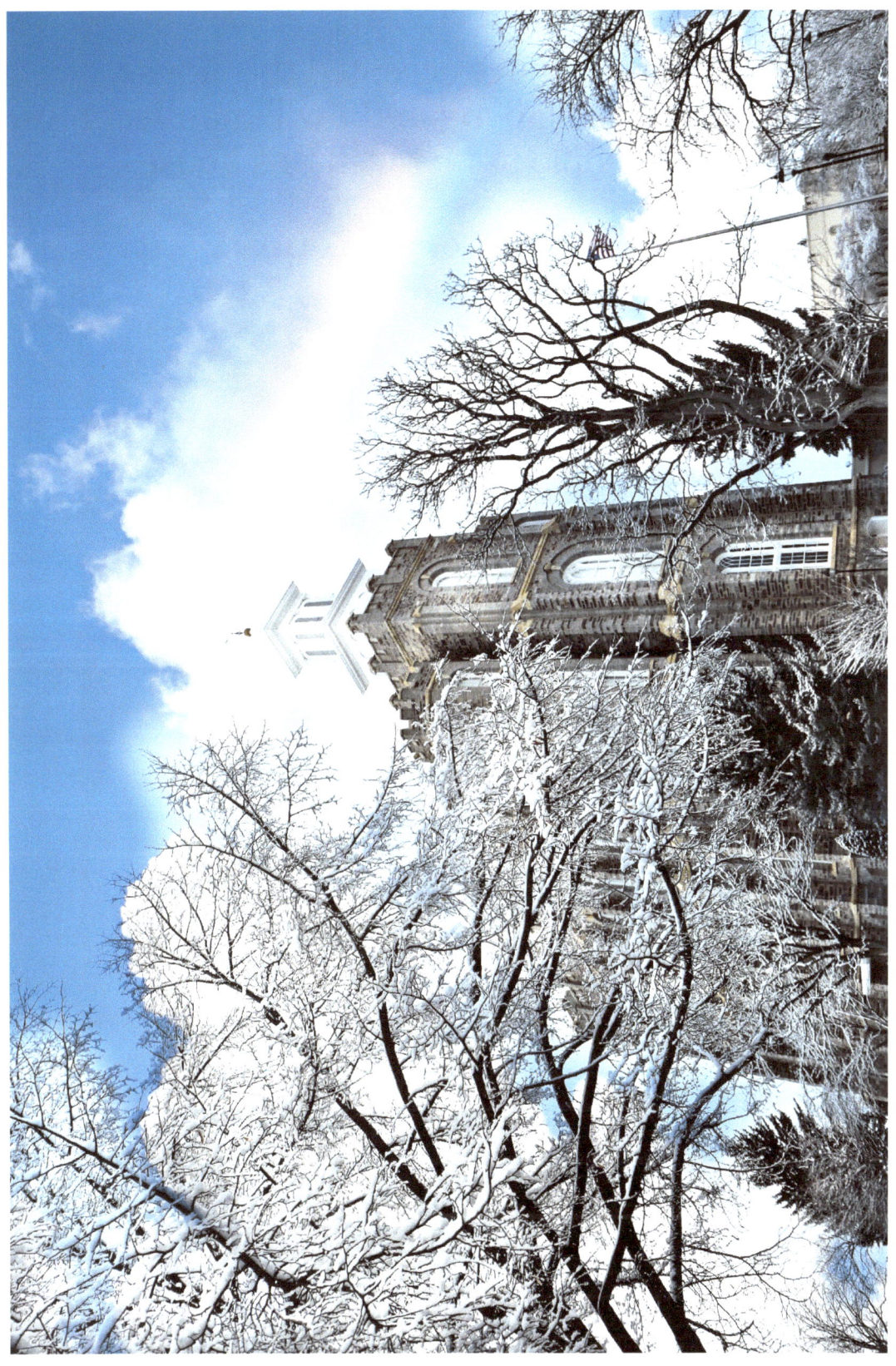

For behold, I have accepted this house,
and my name shall be here; and I will manifest myself
to my people in mercy in this house.

Doctrine & Covenants 110:7

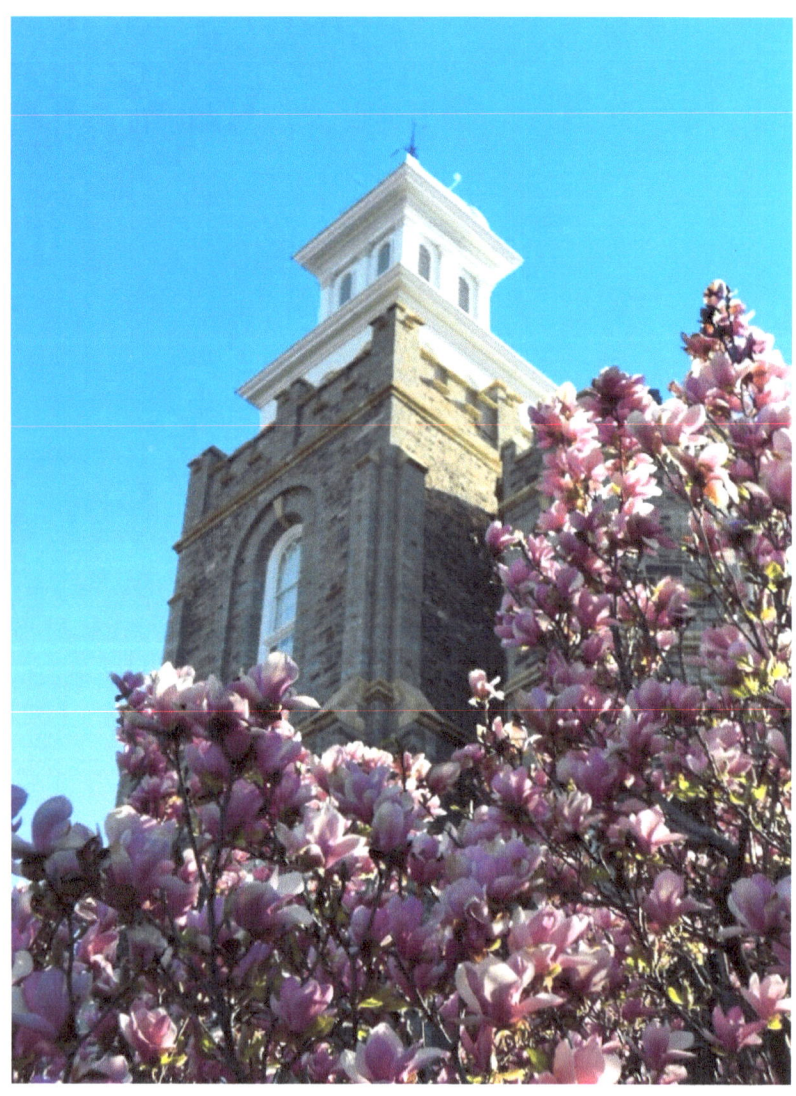

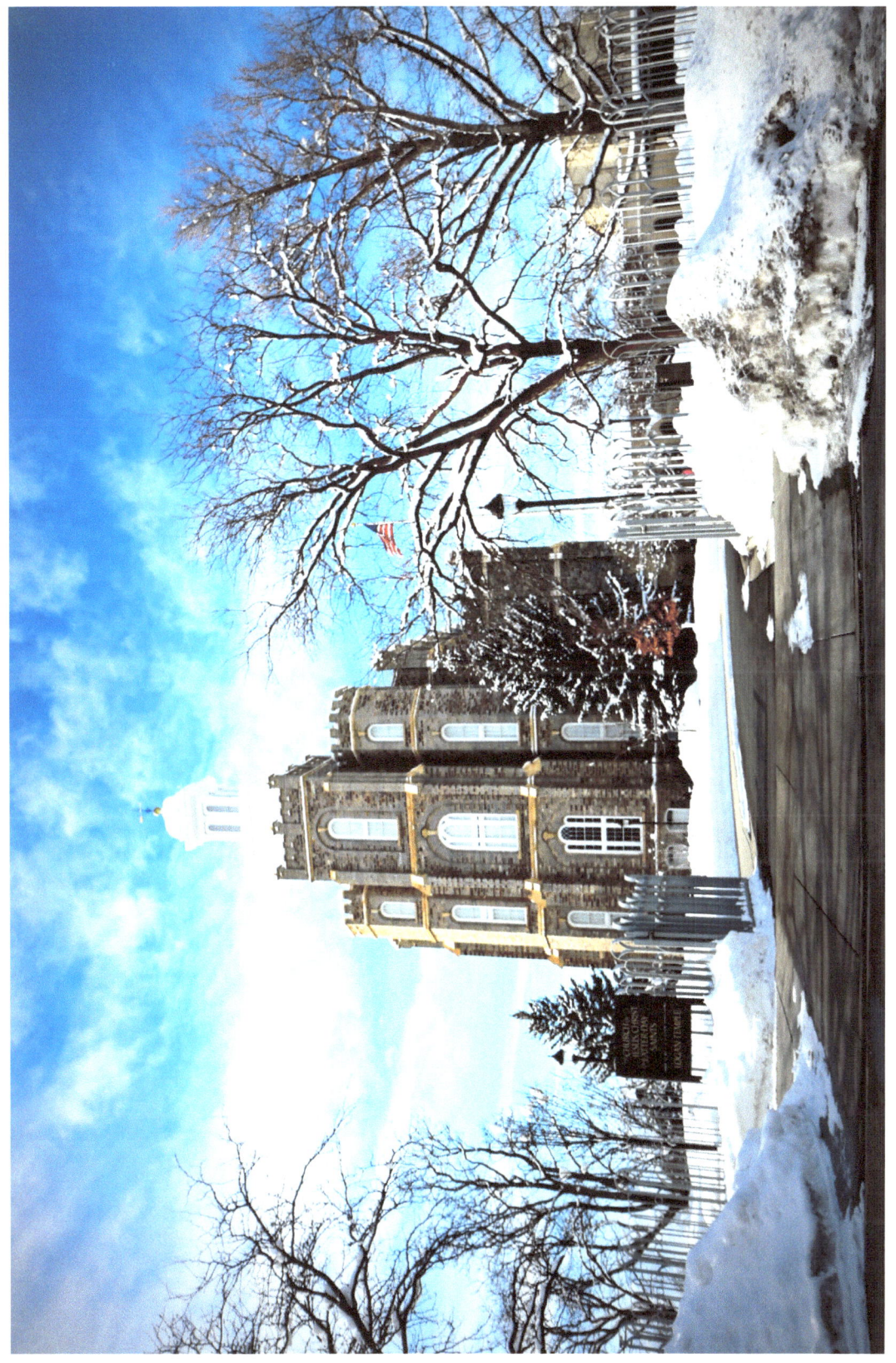

And he reared up the court round about the tabernacle and the altar, and set up the hanging of the court gate. So Moses finished the work.

Then a cloud covered the tent of the congregation, and the glory of the Lord filled the tabernacle.

And Moses was not able to enter into the tent of the congregation, because the cloud abode thereon, and the glory of the Lord filled the tabernacle.

And when the cloud was taken up from over the tabernacle, the children of Israel went onward in all their journeys:
But if the cloud were not taken up, then they journeyed not till the day that it was taken up.

For the cloud of the Lord was upon the tabernacle by day, and fire was on it by night, in the sight of all the house of Israel, throughout all their journeys.

Exodus 40:33-38

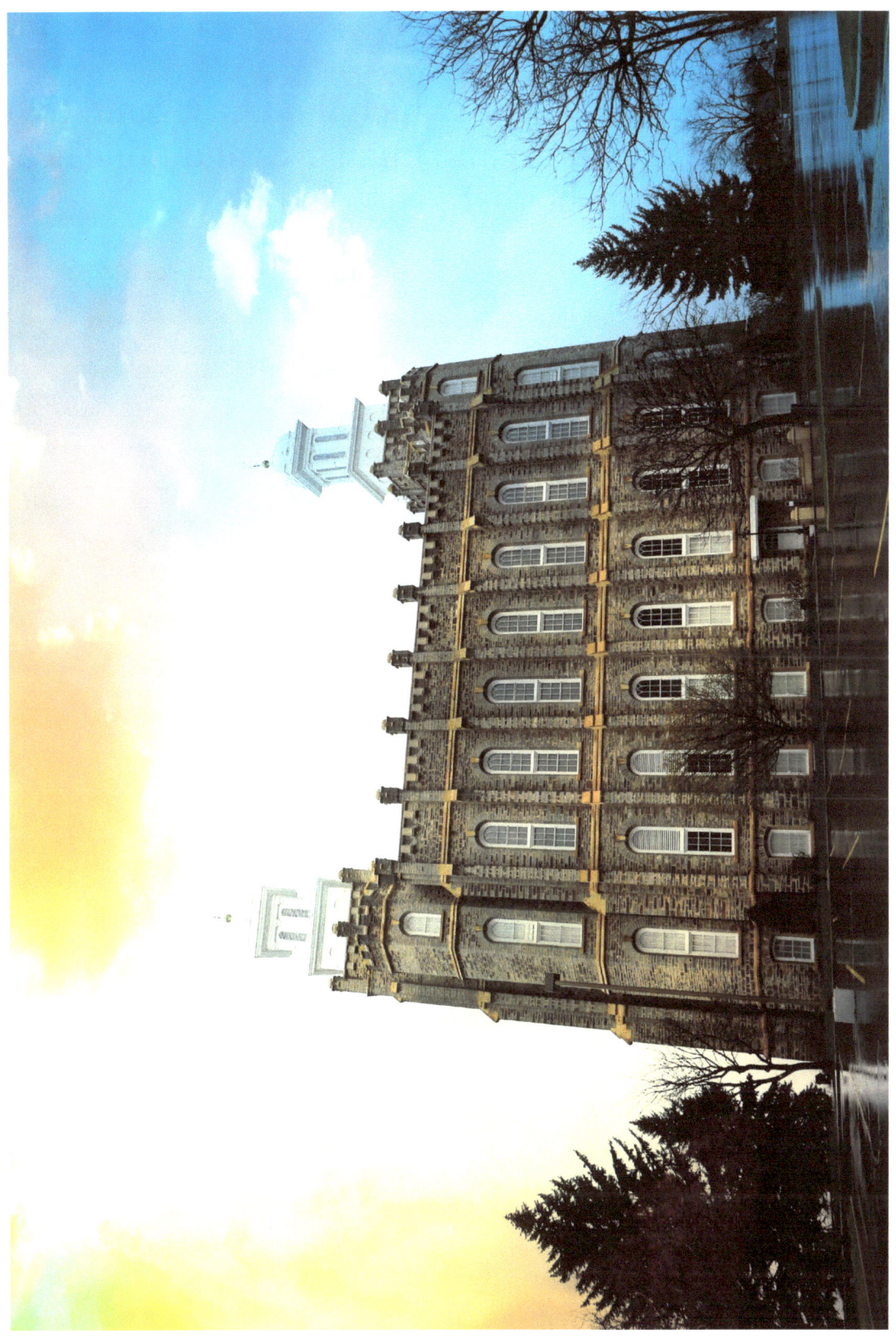

I have hallowed this house, which thou hast built, to put my name there forever; and mine eyes and mine heart shall be there perpetually.

I Kings 9:3

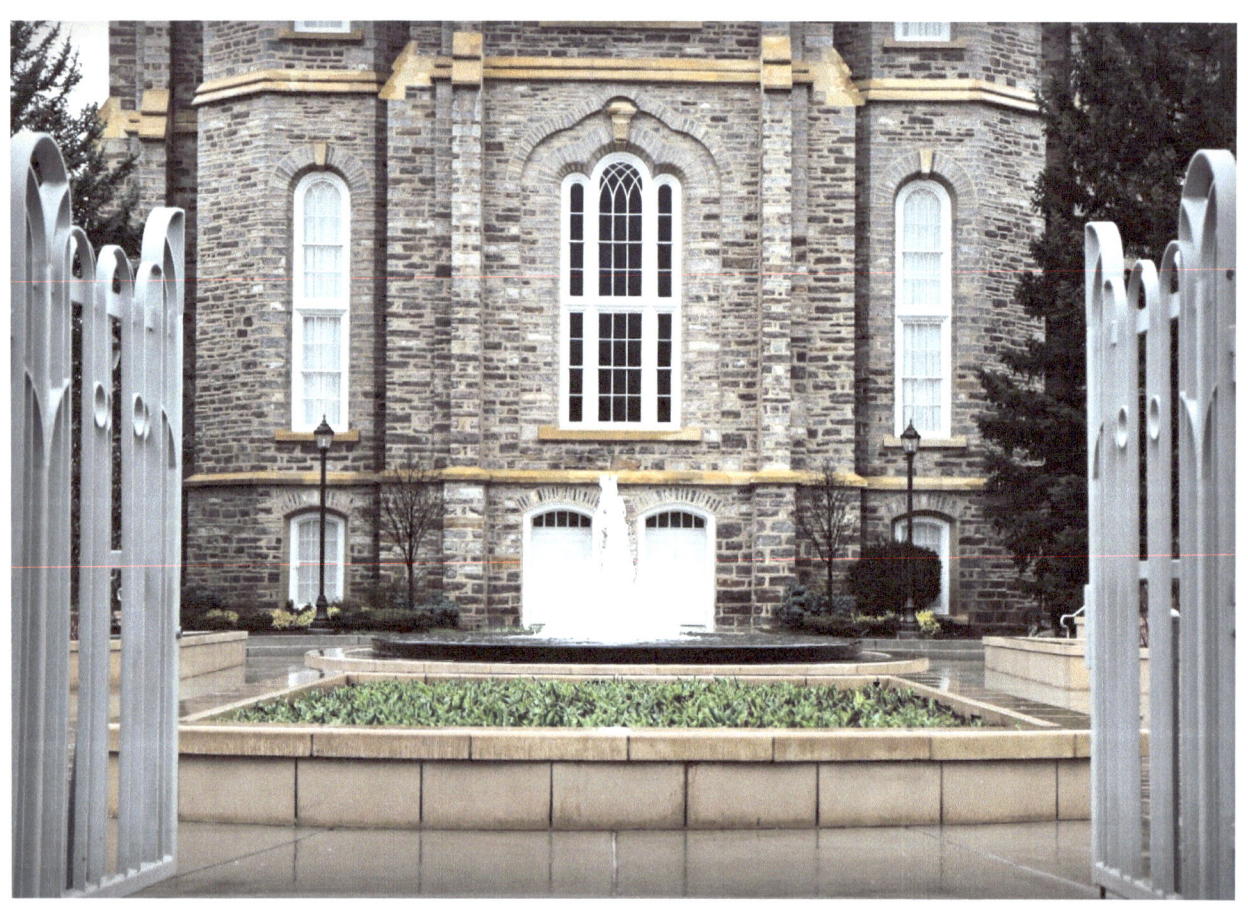

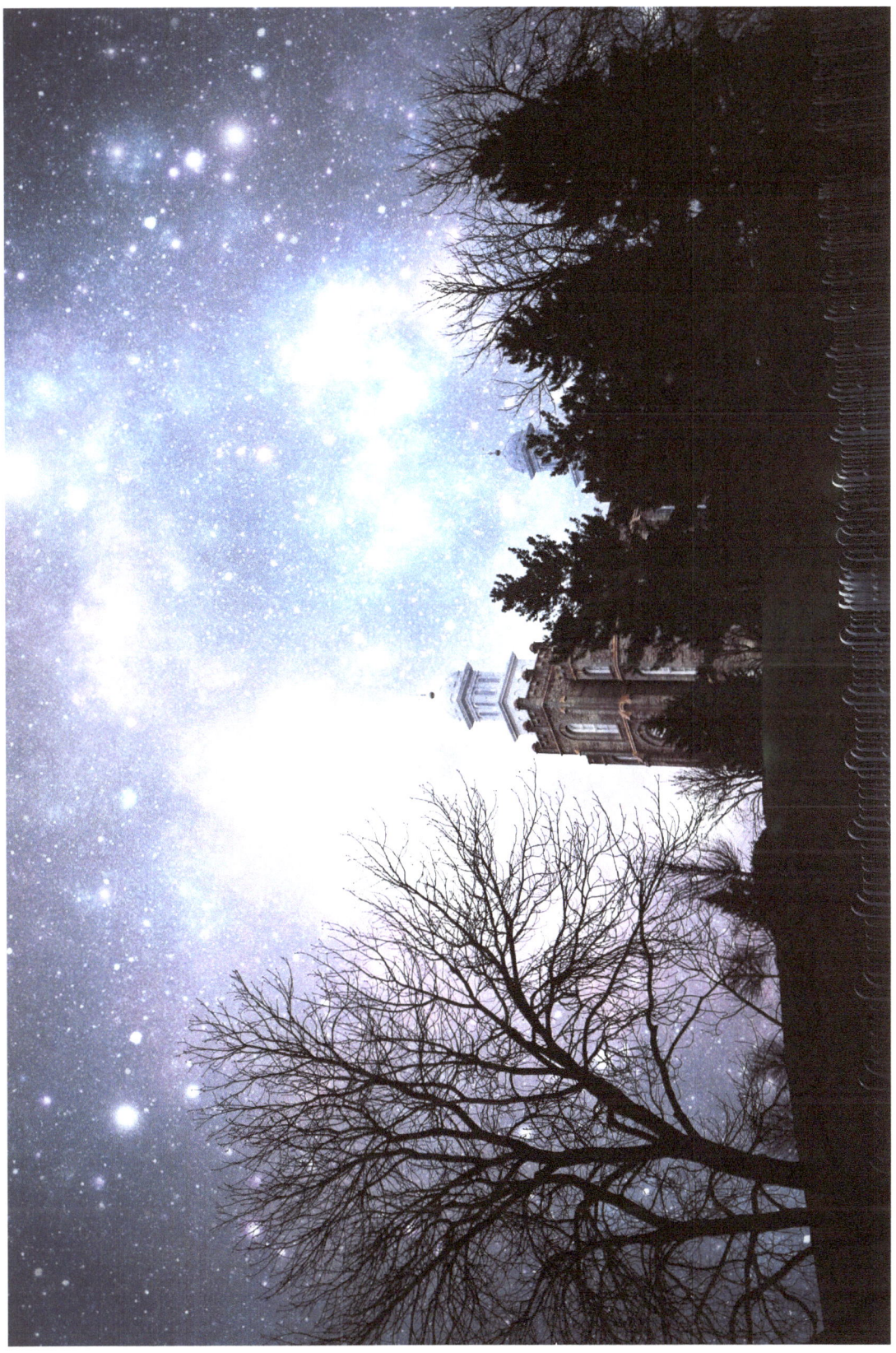

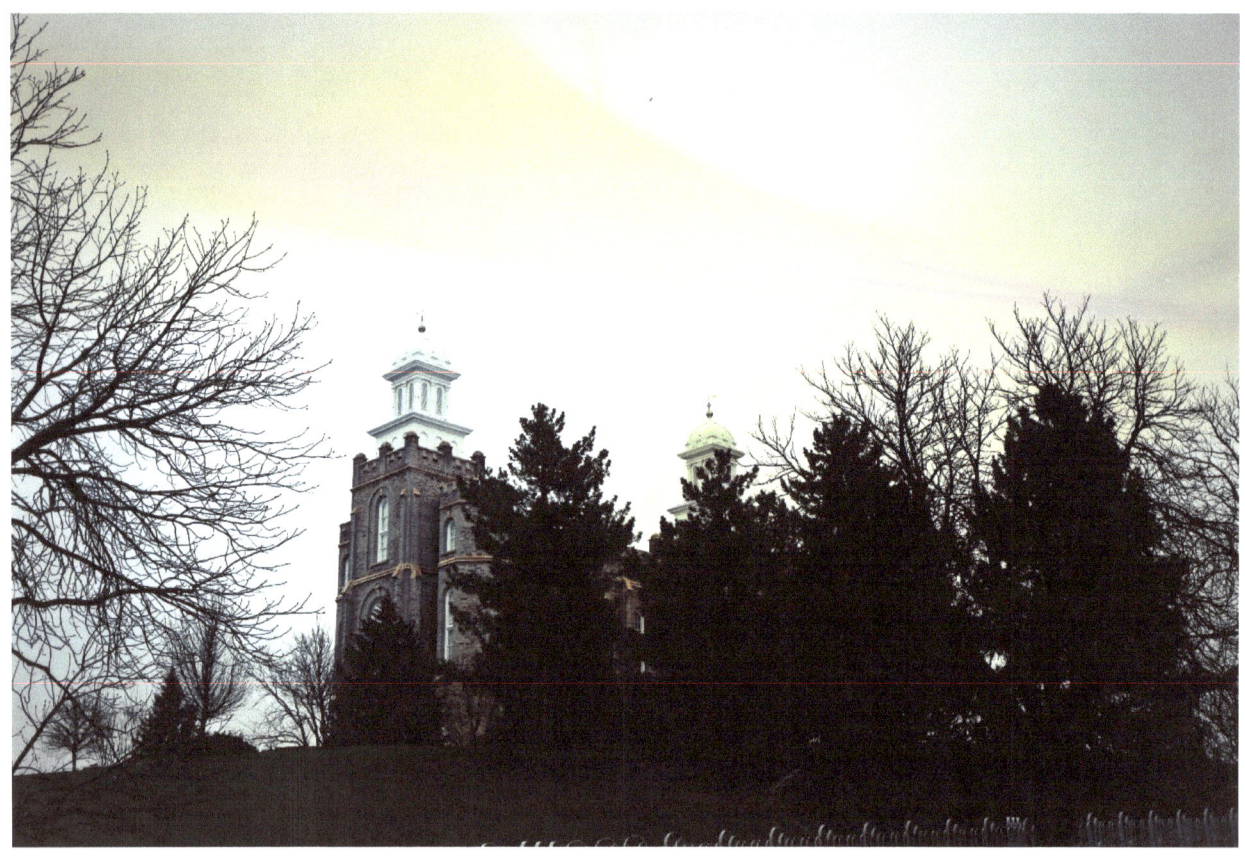

Just as our Redeemer gave His life as a vicarious sacrifice for all men, and in so doing became our Savior, even so we, in a small measure, when we engage in proxy work in the temple, become as saviors to those on the other side.

Gordon B. Hinckley
(Closing Remarks, October 2004)

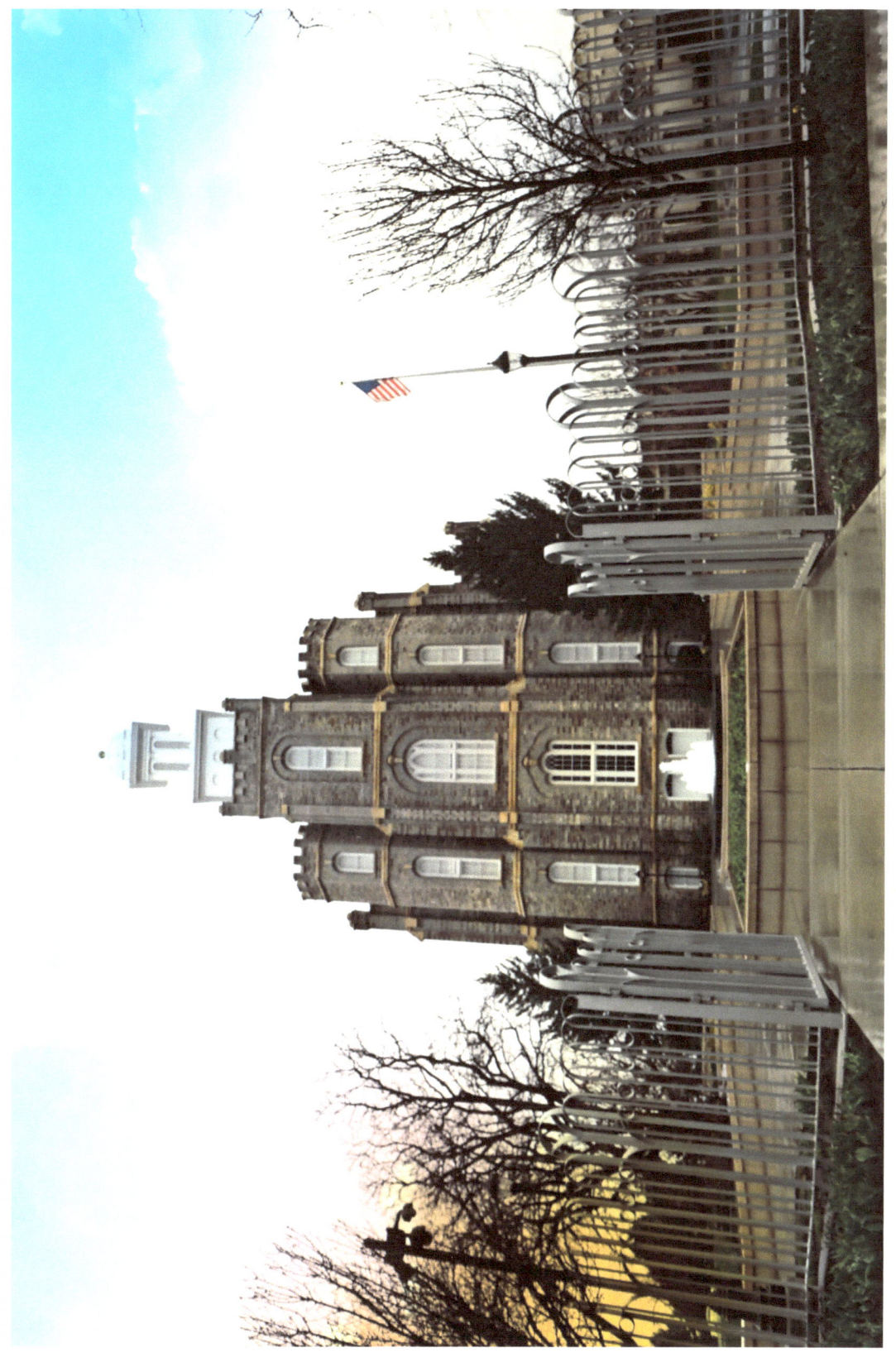

C. A. AYRES

In addition to temples, surely another holy place on earth ought to be our homes. The feelings of holiness in my home prepared me for feelings of holiness in the temple.

James E. Faust
(Standing in Holy Places, April 2005)

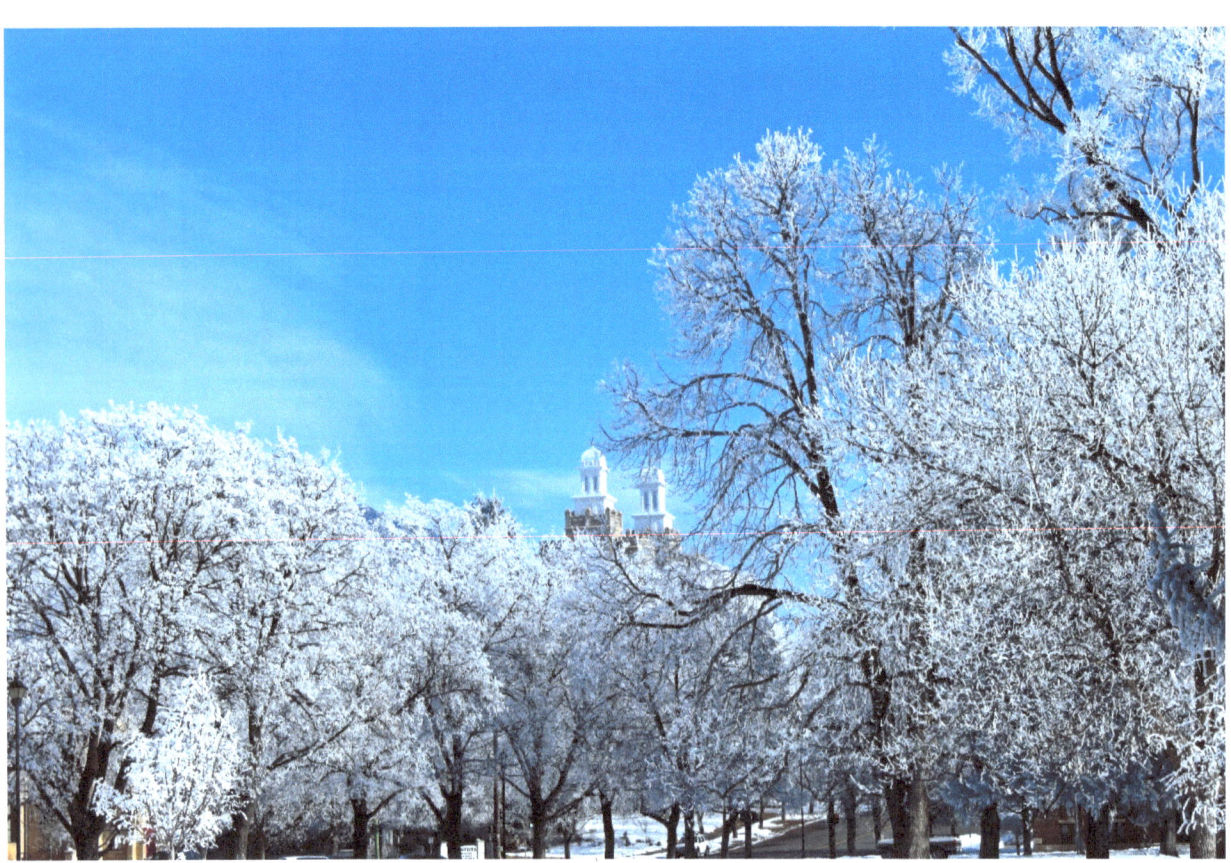

42

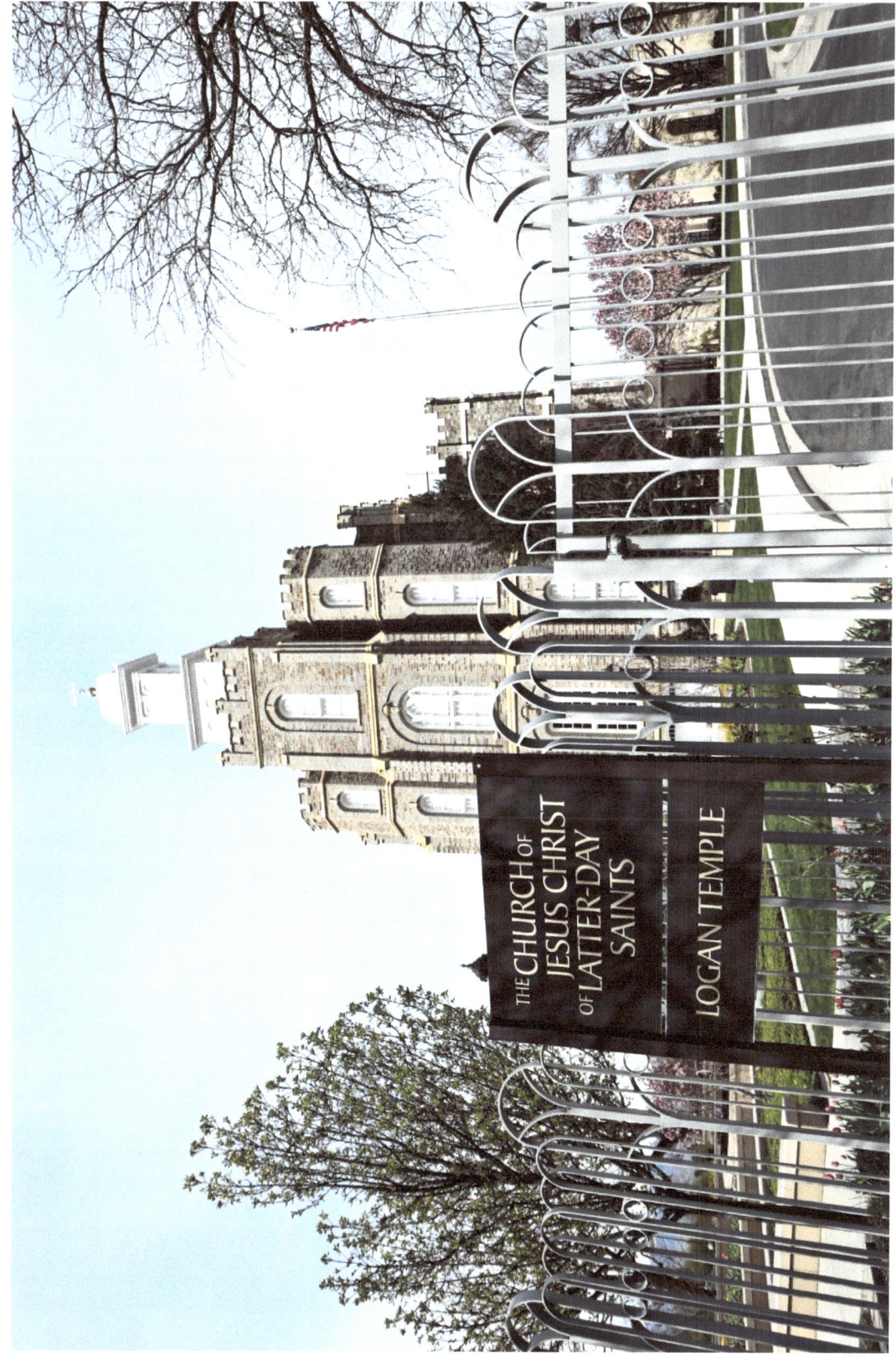

The temple is the house of the Lord. The basis for every temple ordinance and covenant is the Atonement of Jesus Christ. Every activity, every lesson, all we do in the Church, point to the Lord and His holy house.

Russell M. Nelson
(Personal Preparation for Temple Blessings, April 2001)

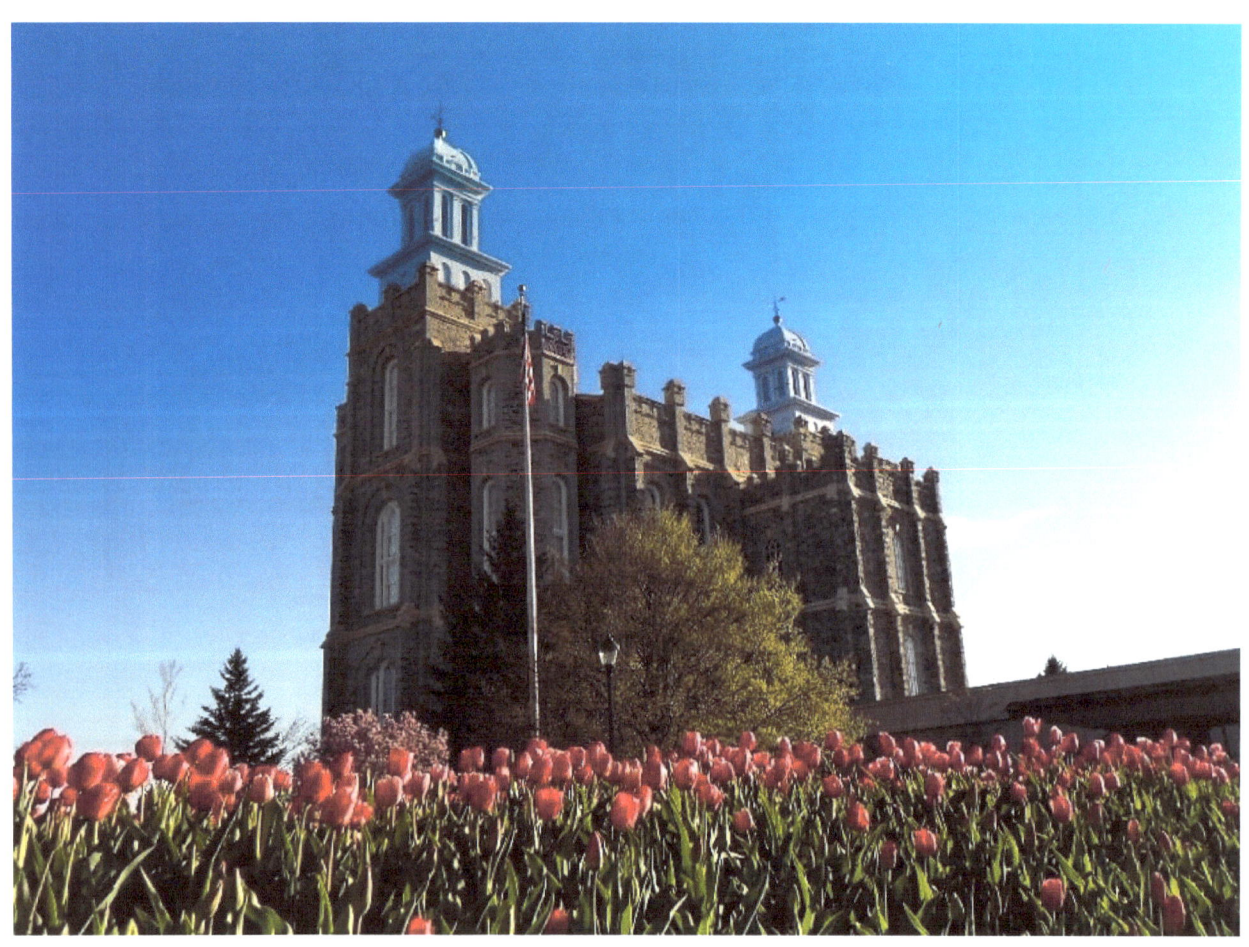

Visit:
http://www.caayresphoto.com/
for more LDS Art.

www.ingramcontent.com/pod-product-compliance
Lightning Source LLC
Chambersburg PA
CBHW051058180526
45172CB00002B/694